Powering the Future

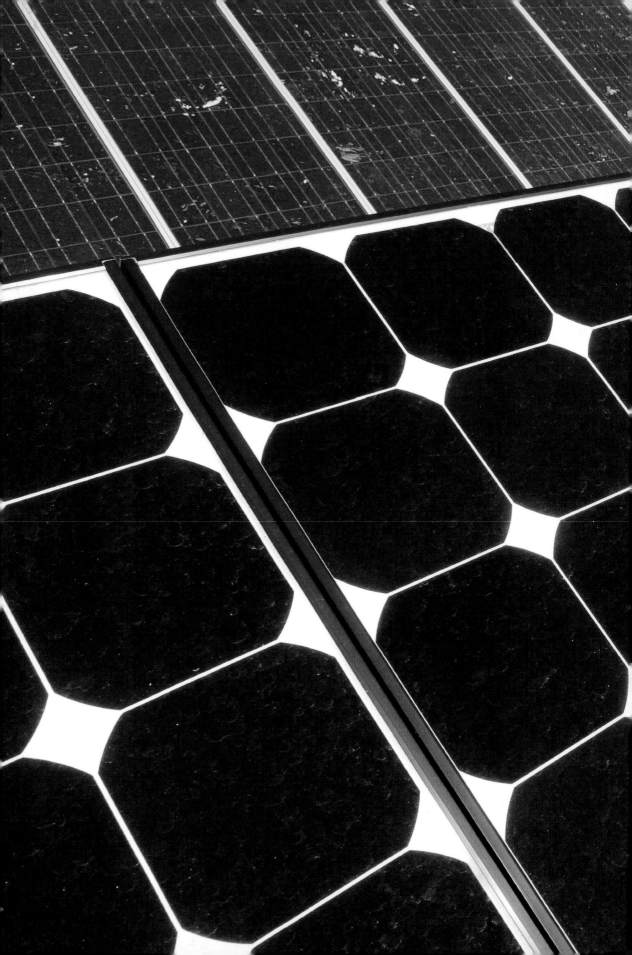

Powering the Future
New Energy Technologies

Eva Thaddeus

with illustrations by Catherine Paplin

University of New Mexico Press | Albuquerque

Barbara Guth Worlds of Wonder

Science Series for Young Readers

Advisory Editors: David Holtby and Karen Taschek

Please see page 121 for more information about the series.

14   13   12   11   10   1   2   3   4   5

LIBRARY OF CONGRESS CATALOGING-IN-PUBLICATION DATA

Thaddeus, Eva, 1965–
Powering the future : new energy technologies / Eva Thaddeus ; with illustrations
by Catherine Paplin.
p. cm. — (Barbara Guth worlds of wonder science series for young readers)
Includes index.
ISBN 978-0-8263-4901-9 (cloth : alk. paper)
1. Renewable energy sources—Juvenile literature. 2. Renewable energy
sources—New Mexico—Juvenile literature. 3. Energy industries—Technological
innovations—New Mexico—Juvenile literature. I. Paplin, Catherine. II. Title.
TJ808.2.T53 2010
333.79'4--dc22
2009044300

For my son and daughter, Benjamin and Anna.
May they live in a time full of new energy.
E. T.

Contents

CHAPTER 1: A World of Energy   1

   Climate in Peril   6

   Spotlight on New Mexico   10

CHAPTER 2: Hotbed of Energy Research   11

CHAPTER 3: Harnessing the Atom   23

   How Nuclear Fission and Fusion Work   32

   Spotlight on France   33

   Nuclear-Powered Spacecraft   34

CHAPTER 4: Energy Under Our Feet   35

   The Story of Fenton Hill   42

   Spotlight on the Philippines   47

CHAPTER 5: Solar Powered   49

   Spotlight on Spain   69

   Spotlight on Germany   69

CHAPTER 6: Reducing Our Use   71

   Spotlight on Japan   89

CHAPTER 7: Weird Fuels on the Way—Or, Can You Power
          a Pickup with Pond Scum?   91

   Spotlight on Brazil   99

CHAPTER 8: Into the Future   101

IF YOU WANT TO KNOW MORE ABOUT POWERING THE FUTURE   107

GLOSSARY   111

ILLUSTRATION CREDITS   119

INDEX   123

CHAPTER 1

A World of Energy

"You can take sunlight and turn it into work, right? That still excites and fascinates me, and I love it." Charles Hanley is talking about solar-electric panels, his specialty. Hanley does research at Sandia National Laboratories in Albuquerque, New Mexico. Two hundred miles (320 kilometers) to the south of him, Wren Stroud discusses a saltwater pond full of dark green *algae* and the people who study it. "We have chemical engineers, we have hydrologists, we have biologists, we have environmental scientists—so if you major in one of those fields when you go to college, you get to look forward to being

Wren Stroud sits in front of a poster that explains the process of turning algae into biodiesel.

a part of something that is maybe going to change the world! How exciting is THAT?"

Hanley and Stroud are two of the many people who work in a happening field. Solar panels and pondweed! Are you asking yourself how these are connected? The connection is *energy*. Hanley and Stroud are both working on developing the energy technologies of the twenty-first century. They are full of energy and excitement themselves because these are the kind of projects that will change life as we know it.

Hanley, Stroud, and their teams think about energy all the time. Most of us think about it sometimes, but it's probably not the first thing on our minds. You may hear people talking about how much we need energy, whether we're running out, how much it costs, and the pollution it causes. But perhaps you've also wondered what the big deal is. It's energy. So what?

Well, imagine this: one weekend you wake up and the power is down in your neighborhood. Your refrigerator doesn't work and the food is starting to get warm. TVs, microwaves, and lightbulbs won't turn on. As the morning goes on, your home starts to get uncomfortable because it's the hottest week of summer and the cooling system doesn't work. How about an electric fan? Not even. Your

Charlie Hanley inspects a photovoltaic panel.

family decides to take a drive out of town in search of some shade and maybe someplace to go swimming. You stop at the nearest gas station, but it's locked up. A sign on the door says, Oil Shortage.

Now you start to understand why energy is such a big deal. If power outages and oil shortages happen often, some of people's basic needs may go unmet. Farms whose machines use oil-based diesel fuel won't be able to operate, and food crops will rot in the fields. Cars, buses, trains, and subways will come to a halt, and many people won't be able to get to work or school. Even water supplies will be threatened if the pumps that operate them break down. The United States hasn't experienced these kinds of problems on a large scale, but other, less-developed countries have. In some places, people have waited in line for hours just to buy a gallon of gas. In some places, the *electricity* only comes on every other day.

In the United States, we're lucky. We have a nation-wide network of electric power lines, known as "the grid," which brings electricity to communities across the country. We have gasoline stations every-where, and our country has never run out of oil. We tend to take our energy supply for granted. Some say we use far too much—with only 5 percent of the world's population, the United States consumes almost 25 percent of the world's energy supply.

So what *is* energy? Energy is defined as the capacity to do work. You could also say that energy is what makes things happen. If some-thing is moving, growing, or changing in any way, then energy is at work. Energy can take many forms and can change from one form to another. Heat, light, sound, and electricity are all forms of *kinetic energy*—meaning energy that moves.

Energy can also be stored, and stored energy is called *potential energy* because it can change back into active energy at any time. In the world of living things, food is the main form of energy storage. When you, or I, or a cat or a cricket eats, we get energy from our

Around the world, human beings are burning fossil fuels at an ever-increasing rate. Courtesy of Geothermal Education Office, Tiburon, CA

food. We use that energy to keep our bodies functioning, to move, and to grow.

When you hear people talking about the "energy" we use, though, they most often mean energy not from food but from fuel. Fuel is an energy source that can be burned, and as you will see in chapter 2, human beings over the course of our history have learned to exploit the potential energy stored in fuel and to burn it in order to produce kinetic energy.

The energy sources that have allowed us to live the way we do today are called *fossil fuels*. The most common of these are *coal*, *petroleum* (also called oil), and natural gas. As their name suggests, fossil fuels come from fossils that have been buried underground for millions of years. For the last 300 years, human beings have been digging up these fuels and burning them. We burn them to give us the energy we need and the energy we want, and we are burning them more and more, faster and faster.

Americans use fossil fuel energy in three main ways. First, we use it in our buildings. Electrical energy runs all the *appliances* we plug into wall sockets. Refrigerators are the appliances that use the most energy year-round, but the little lightbulb is also a big energy consumer because we use so many electric lights. Air conditioners consume a lot of electricity during hot summers. In addition to the electricity, which is usually made from burning coal, many of our buildings use natural gas or home heating oil to provide heat in the winter.

Second, we use energy in our transportation. While our buildings are primarily powered by coal-generated electricity, our transportation today is mostly powered by petroleum, a different fossil fuel. Petroleum products include the gasoline we burn in cars, the diesel we burn in trucks, trains, and buses, and the jet fuel we burn in aircraft.

Third and finally, we use energy to produce our food. *Agriculture* consumes large amounts of energy in the machinery used to prepare fields and in the chemical fertilizers, *pesticides* and *herbicides*

Transmission lines bring electricity from generating plants into communities, where it powers our many plug-in appliances.

Climate in Peril

Coal plants working day and night to give us electricity. Sea ice melting in the Arctic. What could these two things possibly have to do with each other? We can sum up the connection in two words: global warming.

Global warming causes climate change, and a changing climate is something to be concerned about. Climate means the average temperatures, wind, rain, and snowfall characteristic of a place. Southern Florida is hot and wet year-round. New Mexico is hot in the summer, cold in the winter, windy in the spring, and generally dry. The Oregon coast has a warm sunny summer and a cool rainy winter. Every place has its own climate, and these climates tend to stay the same from year to year. But in the distant past, climates were different. A million years ago, most of North America was covered by a large sheet of ice. Fifty million years ago, what is now the desert Southwest was covered by a shallow ocean! We can be reassured that most of these changes took place very gradually, over thousands and even millions of years, not over the course of human lifetimes. But what if the climate did start changing more quickly? Would we notice? What would we do about it?

Climates have begun to change, and we have begun to notice. In 2007, the Northwest Passage in the Arctic was open for the first time in recorded history. This fabled saltwater shortcut from Europe to Asia, which winds its way around the North Pole, was always blocked by ice. For the first time in history, the ice has melted and the passage is open ocean. What is going on?

The good and bad news is that today's climate change is connected to human activity. Good news, because that means we can do something about it. Bad news, because it means changing our way of used to make the crops grow. Transporting the food to processing plants and then to stores is also energy-intensive. The typical piece of food on your plate has traveled hundreds, possibly thousands of miles by boat, train and/or truck before ending up as part of your meal.

Fossil fuels have made it possible for people to develop factories, large-scale farming, automobiles, airplanes, advanced heating and air conditioning, and all our appliances. They have allowed us to live a high-tech way of life that people 300 years ago didn't even dream was possible. But fossil fuels create issues of their own. There are two main problems with fossil fuels. First, they won't last forever. Coal, oil, and gas are non-renewable resources, meaning that they are limited in supply. The faster we use them, the sooner they will run out. Second, burning them causes pollution. The most dangerous pollution we are creating by burning fossil fuels is an excess of *carbon dioxide* in the atmosphere, which is causing *global warming*. Global warming will make temperatures rise and *climates* change all across the world.

The pollution caused by fossil fuels is called an *externality*. This means an unintended consequence of an action. Human beings didn't intend to change the climate

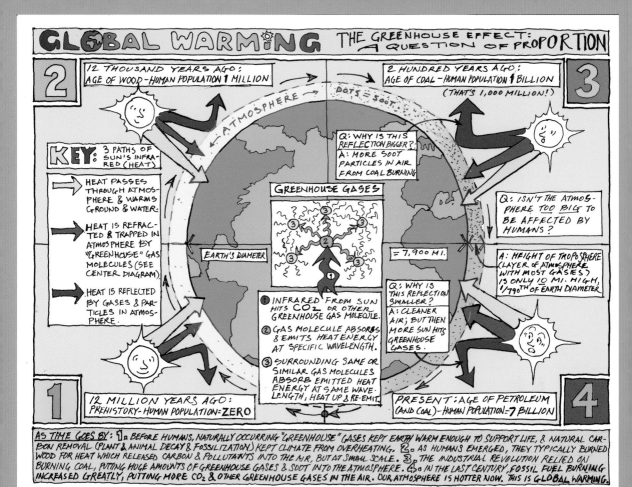

GLOBAL WARMING — THE GREENHOUSE EFFECT: A QUESTION OF PROPORTION

of the globe because of their energy use, yet this is happening and is having an effect on living things that had no choice in the matter. Likewise, people who build coal plants didn't do it to give children asthma, yet more children get asthma when they breathe bad air. We have exploited fossil fuels to get the energy we need and the energy we want, but we have discovered that the externalities of the energy business are causing problems to our long-term health and well-being.

There are alternatives to fossil fuels. In this book, you will read about sources life and moving away from something we depend on. That something is fossil fuels.

The main fossil fuels we use are coal, petroleum, and natural gas. They all come from the remains of living things that were buried underground millions of years ago. Fossil fuels contain carbon, and when carbon is burned, it puts carbon dioxide into the air. Carbon dioxide is a common gas and not poisonous. In fact, it helps make life on earth possible by holding some of the sun's energy in our atmosphere. This action, called the greenhouse effect, warms our planet. Without carbon dioxide and other greenhouse gases, the earth would be an ice-cold, lifeless place.

There is only one problem with the carbon dioxide we are putting into the atmosphere. By burning fossil fuels, we are adding carbon dioxide

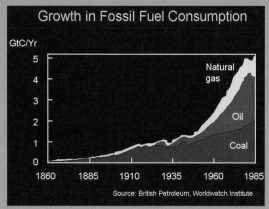

Growth in Fossil Fuel Consumption

GtC/Yr

Natural gas

Oil

Coal

1860   1885   1910   1935   1960   1985

Source: British Petroleum, Worldwatch Institute

The rise in fossil fuel use during the 1900s.

to the atmosphere that didn't used to be there. Remember—that carbon was buried underground for millions of years, and now we are digging it up and putting it into the air. More carbon dioxide increases the greenhouse effect and makes the earth a warmer planet. Around the world, average temperatures have risen 1 degree Fahrenheit (0.5 degree Celsius) in the last 100 years. That isn't much hotter—not yet.

But the human appetite for fossil fuels continues to grow. By burning fossils, we power our automobiles, our planes, our factories, our appliances, our

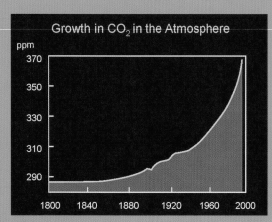

Growth in CO$_2$ in the Atmosphere

ppm

370

350

330

310

290

1800   1840   1880   1920   1960   2000

As fossil fuel use rose, the concentration of carbon dioxide in the atmosphere also rose because whenever fossil fuels are burned, CO$_2$ is released into the air.

furnaces and air conditioners. Our whole economy depends on them. And the global economy keeps getting bigger. China, which manufactures more and more products that the rest of the world buys, is opening a new coal-burning plant every week. Here in the United States, we are just 5 percent of the world's population but burn almost 25 percent

that produce energy without creating bad air or excess carbon dioxide. You may wonder why we continue to burn fossil fuels when these other energy sources already exist. You will discover, as you read on, that this is not a scientific question alone. It's also a question of *economics*—the power of money. For years, fossil fuels have been the cheapest energy source. The cost of their externalities—like the pollution they cause—hasn't been charged to them. What we pay for gasoline is the price of getting the fuel out of the ground, refining and transporting it, plus the profits of the companies that produce it. This price is something people have so far been able to afford. Bear in mind that $3.00, $4.00, even $5.00 a gallon doesn't take into account the cost of asthma or climate change. We pay for those things in other ways—for example, in hospital bills or disaster cleanup after a flood or other extreme weather event.

Advocates for new forms of energy make the case that their favored technologies are also affordable, or will be soon. They make a couple of main points. First, they say, many energy sources would be cost-effective right away if fossil fuels were forced to become responsible for their externalities—that is, if their price reflected all the pollution they cause. Then the price of fossil fuels would go up, and other sources would look better by comparison. In addition, say the advocates, new technologies will become much cheaper just as soon as we invest in them and start to produce them on a large scale. It's a basic law of economics that the more of something you make, the less it tends to cost. So if we get behind new technologies, the price should drop. And we need to get behind these technologies, say the advocates, because the age of fossil fuels is nearly over. We can't continue to mine and drill our energy supply from the ground. The fuels cause too many problems, and besides, they're running low. It's time for a change—a huge change, a transformation of the relationship between human beings and the energy they use.

If the time of fossil fuels is drawing to a close, what will replace them? Where will we get our energy? These are the big questions that will be addressed in this book. You will discover, as you read on, that they are complicated questions. Science is involved. Economics is involved. Politics, and the force of public opinion, are also involved. Some of the people interviewed for this book have strong points of view and advocate for one energy source over others. A lot is at stake here, and the higher the stakes, the stronger the opinions.

of the world's fossil fuel to maintain our way of life. All this activity pours carbon dioxide into the air, and as long as the greenhouse effect increases, the atmosphere will gradually get warmer. This is what is known as global warming.

How will this change life around the world? It's too soon to say for sure. The far northern and southern parts of the world are being affected the most severely, and we already see polar bears and penguins in trouble. But as the world continues to get warmer, other places will change as well. Sea levels will gradually rise, rainfall patterns may shift, and ways of life around the world will have to adapt. Some species, like human beings, are flexible and creative in new situations. But many other species can't take too much change and are likely to go extinct.

A polar bear on a melting ice sheet. Because the Arctic is warming faster than most parts of the world, polar bears are early victims of global climate change.

Climate change threatens all of us. What are we going to do about it? Luckily, because people are the problem, we can also become the solution. Our world needs to move away from fossil fuels and find new sources of energy, and we need to move fast. Will we move fast enough? The next 30 years hold the answer, and that means that people your age will be key to the solution.

Spotlight on New Mexico

In its look at new energy technologies in the United States, this book focuses on one part of the country: New Mexico. New Mexico is a big state with a small population. Large parts of the state are desert, and water supply has always been an issue. But the state has several resources that are moving it into the forefront of the quest for new energy technologies. Those include the natural resources of sun, wind, and geothermal energy and the human resource of scientific expertise. The next chapter will tell the history of the area's long relationship with energy sources and explain how the scientists first came to New Mexico.

We are living in a time of change. This presents us with a challenge, and also an opportunity. Our energy future will look different. How? Charles Hanley, Wren Stroud, and many others are working to answer that question. But their work is just the beginning. The next generation of researchers—your generation—will carry on the quest for technologies to power the future.

A New Mexico landscape.

CHAPTER 2

Hotbed of Energy Research

The Explosion at Trinity Site

Just before dawn, a group of tense and tired scientists huddled in the chilly New Mexico desert. They were waiting for something big to happen. These men had spent the last two years of their lives working urgently on a military project, the most ambitious and frightening venture ever undertaken by science. Now, on July 16, 1945, they were about to find out if their work had succeeded or failed. The world was at war, and the stakes were high.

In the next 30 minutes, two questions would be answered. First, had the scientists succeeded in making a device that would release huge amounts of energy by breaking up atoms into pieces? And second, had the United States just invented the most powerful weapon in the history of the world? Tucked into the back of some scientists' minds was a third question, one they preferred not to think about. Was it possible that all their calculations had been wrong and the explosion once started wouldn't stop? In that case, everything around them might explode—and the atmosphere itself catch on fire. It was a distant possibility, but not a pretty one.

Around the group of people waiting, the scrubby desert extended on all sides, now blue with the first light of morning. Their top-secret work had taken these brilliant minds to the most remote region of the United States, the desert Southwest. To test their new weapon, they had chosen an isolated spot far from humans, which they named Trinity Site. For miles around, the only living beings were jackrabbits and owls, lizards and toads, and the other creatures that made their home in this harsh environment.

Twenty minutes before the scheduled time, a countdown began. The last set of switches was thrown to trigger the explosion. Waiting what they hoped was a safe 10 miles (16 kilometers) from ground zero, the observers felt the time would never pass. They handed around sunscreen in case the explosion burned their skin. A rocket shot up to give a five-minute warning. Then a second rocket, giving a one-minute warning. And then the explosion itself.

First, a light as bright as 20 suns, which lit up the whole horizon. Then a ball of fire, which shot up a mile in the air and grew bigger, changing color from purple, to orange, to green. It's not going to stop, thought some observers. But a few seconds later, the sky was dark again. Then the blast hit them, knocking some people from their feet. It brought heat with it that warmed up the chilly night as if they were standing around a bonfire rather than watching an explosion 10 miles away. "It's beautiful," breathed one. "No, it's terrible," said another.

The project's director, J. Robert Oppenheimer, was interested in Eastern religion and had read many times the Hindu scripture called the Bagawad Gita. As he watched the explosion, his first feeling was relief. The thing worked. Then he thought of a line from the Gita, spoken by the many-armed god Vishnu. He said to himself, "I am become Death, the destroyer of worlds."

It was the dawn of the nuclear age. The first atomic bomb had exploded, and the world would never be the same.

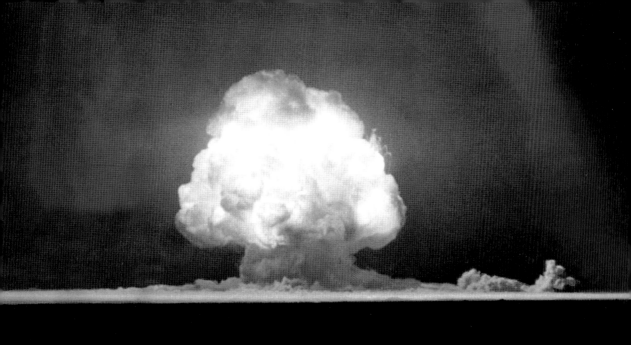

10 SEC.
N

100 METERS

The first atomic explosion took place on July 16, 1945, at Trinity Site in New Mexico. Here, the explosion is seen 10 seconds after ignition.

The Story of Energy in New Mexico

The explosion at Trinity Site changed the relationship between energy and the human race. But the dawn of the nuclear age is just a recent chapter in a long, long story. In fact, as long as human beings have existed on earth, we have made use of energy. What kinds of ancient uses of energy jump to your mind?

Let's look at New Mexico, the birthplace of the Trinity Site, as our example. The land now called New Mexico is part of the south-western United States, a sunny, rugged part of North America that looks and feels like a difficult place to live. It's hot in the summer, cold in the winter, and dry year-round. But in spite of its difficult climate, people have lived in this land for over 10,000 years. The original inhabitants were hunter-gatherers. They killed animals and collected plants for food.

Food is the number-one source of energy for all members of the animal kingdom. Because animals must eat to stay alive, finding food is a basic instinct. People, of course, are animals too, and we share this instinctive need for nourishment. Our bodies digest the food we eat and use it to grow, move, and stay warm. In this way, we are just like other animals. But unlike any other animal, human beings have discovered how to use energy in many different ways. The most important discovery of all, and one of the earliest, was the taming of fire.

Anasazi cliff dwellings were built facing south to take advantage of winter sunlight that gave the rooms light and warmth. This photograph of an ancient doorway in Bandelier National Monument was taken in early spring, a time of year when the sun still hits the doorway. In the summer, south-facing rooms are mostly in shade.

Using Fire and the Sun

Many cultures have ancient stories that tell how people first got fire. Tribes native to the Southwest say that Coyote stole it from the Fire people or that the Badger people kept it at the center of a great shell. Charcoal found near ancient dwellings tells scientists that people have been burning wood as far back as we can trace. And we are the only

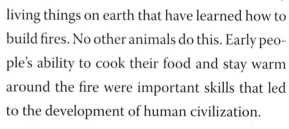

living things on earth that have learned how to build fires. No other animals do this. Early people's ability to cook their food and stay warm around the fire were important skills that led to the development of human civilization.

In New Mexico, native peoples used what is called a fire drill to start their fires. Spinning a small piece of wood between their palms, they let it rub against another piece of wood as it twirled. The energy created by the friction ignited sparks, which then set ablaze small piles of bark shavings. If you have ever tried to use a fire drill yourself, you know it takes a great deal of skill and patience. The native

CLIFF DWELLING in SUMMER

SUN AT NOON IN SUMMER IS AT A HIGH ANGLE, LEAVING THE INTERIOR MOSTLY IN SHADE

CLIFF DWELLING in WINTER

SUN AT NOON IN WINTER IS AT A LOW ANGLE, ALLOWING SUN'S RAYS TO PENETRATE DEEPLY INTO THE DWELLING

people of New Mexico were masters of the survival skills needed to live in their difficult environment.

Native people in the sunny Southwest also learned to use *solar energy* to help them heat their homes. If you visit the famous cliff dwellings of Mesa Verde in Colorado or Bandelier National Monument in New Mexico, you will see that the rooms are built into a rock wall horses, mules, and oxen. After the steam engine was invented, people's ability to work expanded dramatically. So they invented new kinds of transportation, built factories, and grew their cities. All of this depended on the work of the steam engine, and what did the steam engine depend on? It burned coal. The more Europe grew its economy, the more coal it needed and the more coal it mined.

It wasn't until the 1800s that the Industrial Revolution reached New Mexico, which was still part of Mexico at the time. The area turned out to be rich in coal. Coal mines were dug. After the United States took over in 1848, a major railroad called the Santa Fe Railway was built across New Mexico, and its trains were fueled by coal. The towns where the trains stopped—Raton, Albuquerque, Belen, and others—grew in population. Immigrants of European background now outnumbered the Native Americans in the territory called New Mexico. It was entering the modern age, fueled by industrial-strength energy.

Age of the Automobile

New Mexico became a state of the United States in 1912. Shortly afterward, the state began to produce oil. Oil! This was the new, hot source of energy, the one that powered a sensational new technology called the automobile. Oil, also known as petroleum, is a fossil fuel like coal. But unlike coal, it's a liquid, and the way it burns made new kinds of technology possible. The internal combustion engine replaced the steam engine. This allowed Henry Ford to develop and market the first car, the Model T. The southwestern United States turned out to be the most oil-rich part of the world. Suddenly, America was rich in energy, and Americans were driving.

The invention of the car transformed human society once more. Cities spread out. Highways were paved. Regions were interconnected with a network of roads. In the United States, ordinary people

Route 66, the first cross-country highway in the United States, still exists. The old-fashioned sign of this motel in Albuquerque, New Mexico, celebrates the history of Central Avenue as part of the original cross-country route for motorists. More "old Route 66" architecture is visible in the background.

could own cars and travel long distances. Route 66, which passes through New Mexico, became the first cross-country highway, and the "road trip" was born.

This brings us back to the middle of the twentieth century, when World War II turned human society upside down and the atomic bomb was invented at Los Alamos. Where would New Mexico go from here? It would become a hotbed of energy research.

natural resources of plentiful sun and wind—two energy sources that may play a big role in our future—and you have a state that many people envision as a high-energy center of the world. What a change from a century ago, when most of New Mexico's roads were dirt and many of its homes were still heated by wood-burning stoves.

CHAPTER 3

Harnessing the Atom

The Birth of Nuclear Power

After the end of World War II, the government of the United States encouraged the development of *nuclear energy* for peaceful purposes. The Atomic Energy Commission was created in 1946, and construction began on the world's first *nuclear reactor*. In Idaho, in 1951, it generated the first electricity ever produced from nuclear fission. The reactor was so small it could only power four lightbulbs.

Many people had high hopes for nuclear power because fission can produce such huge amounts of energy. The United States moved quickly to develop the world's first large-scale nuclear reactors. *Uranium*, a radioactive element, was mined to provide the fuel. Other countries followed. By the 1970s, nuclear reactors were producing power in many parts of the world. A nuclear power plant works like any other steam-electric *generator*. It makes heat to boil water, which turns to steam. The steam turns a *turbine* that produces electricity. A nuclear plant was able to produce as much electricity as a coal plant, and its fuel appeared to be cleaner. People had high hopes that nuclear energy would become so cheap it was almost free. But a couple of things happened to put the brakes on the nuclear power *industry*. Have you heard of any of these things?

First, uranium turned out to have problems as a fuel. A large number of the miners who first dug the uranium got sick because exposure

Reactor Safety

Sandia National Laboratories in Albuquerque is one of the centers of research into nuclear reactor safety. Marshall Berman, a physicist, spent almost 20 years studying nuclear safety and has this to say: "When I got involved, the first area I worked in was building a computer model of a reactor, and I deliberately did bad things to the model to see what would happen. For example, what if the main water lines feeding the reactor simply came apart?" Berman explains that overheating is the main threat to the safety of a reactor and that water is used to keep it cool. All nuclear reactors, at least through the 1970s, were designed with two safety systems. One was called the emergency core cooling system. That used power to drive water back into the reactor core to keep it cool. But in the case of a loss of power, there was a second system, a huge tank of water above the reactor that would fall into the reactor by gravity if the reactor overheated.

Berman and his colleagues went on to consider disasters worse than power loss—for example, a terrorist attack or natural disaster. "I and many others became proponents of super-strong containment buildings. The reactor building is very strong, but we thought, well, what if you crashed an airplane into it or a monstrous earthquake occurs. A colleague of mine in fact ran an impact test. They took a sample of concrete and ran a fighter jet into it, and there are films of that—a fighter jet speeding right into the wall. The plane just crumples and that's it, with a few nicks in the wall. This test was part of a large effort at Sandia to investigate the responses of nuclear reactor containment buildings to threats."

Berman discusses the accident at Three Mile Island. "It was an amazing situation. We studied it for a long time after the accident, and it was caused by something the engineers hadn't thought of." That something was major human error. The operators in charge of the plant didn't understand what was happening. "Despite the fact that all the alarm bells were ringing, that the core cooling system kept trying to kick in and the gravity valves were trying to open, the operators kept shutting them all down and refused to believe that they were having problems." What actually caused the accident was a stuck-open valve. Berman says, "The reactor operators turned a small problem into a major event by doing almost all the wrong things. The reactor boiled dry, and I think about half the core melted into a big lump inside the reactor. There was no shock wave and no explosion. No one was hurt, and no significant radiation was released, and there was no real threat to the public at all, except for fear, but there was lots of fear." Berman thought at the time that if nuclear reactor operators were going to make such bad mistakes, safety systems should be designed so that even the operators couldn't shut them down. Now, he says, a new design does that. "If the temperature rises above a

Water is used to cool nuclear reactors so they don't overheat. This is why nuclear power plants release steam when they are in operation.

certain point, the operator is out of the picture and the safety features kick in."

Berman is convinced that after 54 years of experience, knowledge, and redesign, new reactors are safe. He believes that nuclear energy is safer than energy from coal plants. He says the death toll at Chernobyl was small compared to the deaths caused by coal-fired power plants, and he gives numbers: an estimated 5,000 coal miners die every year on the job, 25,000 people in the United States alone die yearly of respiratory illnesses related to air pollution from coal, and "more uranium comes out of coal stacks in a year than is used in nuclear power plants." Not to mention global-warming pollution in the form of carbon dioxide, which is produced in huge quantities by coal plants and not at all by nuclear plants. About waste disposal, Berman says, "In my opinion, Yucca Mountain is incredibly safe and what's going on now is totally political, has nothing to do with science and engineering." For really big power plants, he says, "Right now there are only two choices, coal and nuclear, and I'm way over on the nuclear side. I think coal has too many environmental problems with it."

As you can begin to see, discussions about energy may turn into debates. People take sides, with advocates in favor of certain sources and critics opposing them. What kind of things are most important as we consider our energy future? This is a big question for all of us.

Working Toward a Hydrogen Economy

John Kelly is another Sandia engineer who does nuclear research. "My work," he says, "is looking at the future, where are we going to be 20 years from now. That's what's most exciting to me. Not just getting electricity, but—what other things can we use nuclear power for?"

Kelly is interested in making hydrogen-fueled transportation a reality. A lot of people are interested in hydrogen these days. It's the lightest element, number 1 on the periodic table. It burns cleanly without polluting, creating only water as a by-product. The National Aeronautics and Space Administration (NASA), the branch of the U.S. government in charge of space exploration, has used hydrogen fuel in its spacecraft for years. The space shuttle runs on hydrogen and oxygen. Many people envision a "hydrogen economy" of the future where hydrogen tanks replace gas tanks as hydrogen becomes the main fuel.

Kelly says, "We're trying to figure out how best to do it. We have some experiments going on right now. There are probably four main elements of working toward a hydrogen economy. One is produc-tion—how you make the hydrogen. Next one is how you ship it. Then how you store it in a vehicle, then how the vehicle converts the hydro-gen into electricity. We know how to do that, but the issue is cost. It's just very expensive. Storage is a difficult issue because hydrogen is very light—if you want to have a car go 300 miles [480 kilometers], you'd need to have a lot of hydrogen. If you store it as a gas, it would be under high pressure, and people worry that if you're in a crash, the gas could get out and burn, and you'd have a big problem. People at Sandia are working on all these things."

Opposite page: Sandia National Laboratories in Albuquerque has carried out many tests related to the safety of nuclear reactors. This series of photographs shows a test designed to determine the impact force of an F-4 Phantom jet on a massive concrete structure. The jet is shown hitting the concrete wall at 480 miles per hour (772 kilometers per hour) and exploding. The test established that the major impact force was from the engines.

NASA's space shuttle is powered by hydrogen fuel cells. Advocates of nuclear energy say it would be a good future source of the power needed to manufacture hydrogen fuel.

Managing the Waste Stream

As we saw above, the radioactivity of nuclear fuel and nuclear waste is what makes this form of energy so controversial. Many nuclear scientists and advocates want our country to move toward re-using (reprocessing) nuclear waste instead of burying it. The spent fuel rods that come out of the reactor still have uranium and fissionable plutonium in them and can be reprocessed and used again. Kelly says nuclear waste is bulky and so, "If we're looking at expanding the amount of nuclear power, we have to pay a lot more attention to how we get rid of the waste." What to do with all that new waste? "You would need to take the waste and the spent fuel, chop it up, dissolve it, then separate out the good stuff. If you did this in an effective way, you could reduce the amounts of waste. It's an idea that's been around for a while. Other nations like France and Japan are doing recycling of spent fuel already."

In the United States, the idea of fuel reprocessing is also controversial. Critics raise the possibility that nuclear material will be lost or stolen if it's not kept secure. They don't like the thought of potent radioactive fuel traveling by truck from one location to another. But recently, the U.S. government decided that reprocessing fuel can take place. The discussion about the future of nuclear energy continues. Can it be safe enough? Advocates say it already is. Critics doubt it ever will be.

The Promise of Nuclear Fusion

Nuclear fission, which means the splitting apart of atoms, is one way that elements can change into other elements and release energy. But it's not the only way. The opposite process—when two atoms combine into a bigger one—is known as nuclear fusion. The fusion of two hydrogen atoms into a helium atom is the energy source of the sun and the other stars. It's what makes them burn. This fusion process produces more energy than fission. For years now, scientists have had hopes of copying this process on earth. Nuclear fusion could be the source of huge amounts of clean energy. Could it solve all our energy problems?

Marshall Berman remembers the early years of high hopes about fusion. "You know, I was so excited about fusion when I got my PhD, and that was 1968. So here we are now, 40 years later, and in my opinion, we're still 50 years out from a controlled fusion reaction. It turns out to be incredibly difficult." What is so hard about it? "You have to develop something like the sun in a small location." The center of the real sun is under very high pressure and temperature because of its huge mass and huge gravity. In this pressure-cooker environment, hydrogen atoms are slammed into each other at very high speeds, which is what makes them fuse. But there is no environment this extreme on earth. Here, in order to create such high pressures,

How Nuclear Fission and Fusion Work

Nuclear fission is the process of breaking an atom's nucleus apart.

• The nucleus of an atom contains protons and neutrons.

• Every element has a different number of protons. Elements with different numbers of neutrons are called *isotopes* of the same element.

• Hydrogen—with one proton—is the smallest and lightest of the elements.

• The heavier an atom is, the more likely it is to have unstable isotopes. Some unstable elements (like uranium) if hit by a neutron will break apart, releasing energy and more neutrons.

• These neutrons can bump into other unstable atoms, breaking them. If enough atoms are present in a small space, more and more fission leads to what is called a nuclear chain reaction, which releases an enormous amount of energy in a very short time.

• Radioactivity means the particles released by an unstable nucleus.

Nuclear fusion is the combining of two atoms into one.

• Fusion is the energy source of the sun and the other stars.

• Inside the sun, hydrogen atoms are exposed to tremendously high temperatures and pressure. Under these conditions, they slam into one another and combine to form helium.

• The fusion process continues with the formation of bigger elements up to iron.

• Fusion releases a large amount of energy. This is what causes the sun to burn. It can only continue under conditions of high temperature and pressure.

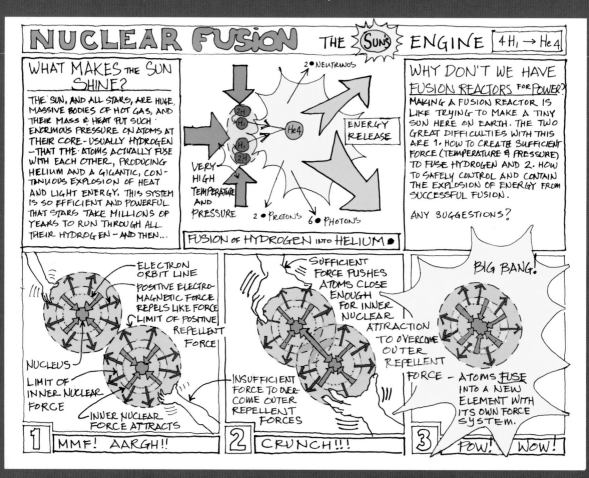

scientists have to use a lot of energy. Berman says, "Yeah, you can cause it to happen, but it takes more energy than you get out of it, so right now it's not a practical system. It's been tried only on a very small scale."

When asked if he expects fusion to become practical anytime soon, Kelly says, "It's hard to tell. I think it's going to come down to cost. The problem is it takes some fairly exotic materials that can withstand these temperatures and pressures." Although the science can be shown to work, it will be hard to engineer a system that is cost-effective. "I think it's going to take a long time. Maybe some breakthroughs in nanotechnology, where we learn how to make better materials, are going to be necessary."

Meanwhile, an international project aims to show that fusion power is feasible. The name of this project is ITER, and it's a cooperative enterprise of the European Union, Japan, China, India, South Korea, Russia, and the United States. The ITER project will be in France. It's intended to be the first plant that produces electricity generated by nuclear fusion. According to the ITER website, the long-term goal of the project is to demonstrate that fusion can produce electricity safely and "meet the needs of a growing world population."

Nuclear energy is a huge source of energy in the universe. Here on earth, power from fission is affordable today, but questions continue to be raised about the safety of radioactive fuel and waste. Critics say that if the cost of these externalities were included, nuclear energy would no longer be affordable. Energy from nuclear fusion would bypass these concerns, but fusion has not yet proven to be affordable or realistic. What role will nuclear energy play in your own future? The question remains to be answered, but we know this much: nuclear power is a force to be reckoned with.

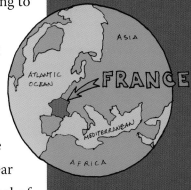

Nuclear-Powered Spacecraft

Have you ever wondered how spacecraft are powered? There are three ways: chemical batteries, solar panels, and nuclear power. Power is needed to produce electricity so the spacecraft can take pictures, run instruments, and communicate with planet Earth. Solar panels work to power the two Rovers on Mars, but the Rovers also have small radioisotope power sources on board, which are small nuclear devices. These are needed to keep the electronics warm during the cold Mars nights.

If we ever hope to explore the dark side of the moon, John Kelly says nuclear power will be our best option. And he goes further. "If humans are actually going to explore the solar system and go back to the moon and eventually go on to Mars, at some point we're going to need nuclear reactors on the moon and on Mars." He says the reactors on other planets would be different from the ones we have on Earth. They would be smaller. For one thing, it's hard to send building materials into space, and we couldn't send a lot. For another, we wouldn't need big energy production there. We would need reactors big enough to power our spacecraft and create new fuel for them. "If you could find water on the moon—and there is some evidence that there's ice on the dark side—you could bring a reactor to make hydrogen and oxygen, the exact things that rocket fuel is made of. This is cool stuff. If we put our mind to it, in 50 years we could be exploring the moon in this fashion and perhaps going to Mars."

Now Kelly puts out an idea that's even wilder. "I'll tell you the problem with going to Mars. To go to Mars in a chemically powered rocket takes two years. In this case, nuclear has a different option, and it's called nuclear-thermal propulsion. And the idea is that you could use a nuclear reactor to heat gases to very high temperatures. You could send out those hot gases through a thruster nozzle at the end of the rocket, and get up to very high speeds, and cut your travel time down to a few months." Why nuclear power? For its mass, nuclear fuel produces much more energy than chemical fuel—almost a million times as much. So the small amount of fuel that you can actually take into space would make more energy and get you to Mars faster.

Kelly says, "The idea is that the astronauts would need lots of supplies, so two years in advance of their landing, you would send all the supplies on chemical rockets. And then you would use the nuclear system to transport the astronauts. That's some of the thinking that's going on. These are some exciting uses of nuclear energy."

Above: An artist's rendering of a Mars Exploration Rover. This Rover contains a small nuclear power source that keeps its electronic equipment warm.

CHAPTER 4

Energy Under Our Feet

Where does energy on the earth come from? Trick question. You might say the sun, and you'd be mostly right. Most of the energy that is readily available on this planet is either directly or indirectly solar. It's the sun that makes life possible on earth. But not all of our energy comes from the sun. Look at the photograph on this page. These people, who are soaking in a natural hot spring, are enjoying energy from a source that *isn't* solar. That energy source is the topic of this chapter.

Geothermal energy comes from the earth's core. The word *geothermal* derives from two Greek words, *geo*, meaning "earth," and *therme*, meaning "heat." At the center of our planet, temperatures are as high as 9,000 degrees Fahrenheit (F.) (5,000 degrees Celsius, C.)—which is hotter than the surface of the sun. The story of how this heat got inside our planet goes back over four billion years. When our solar system formed, Earth and the other planets were fiery balls of red-hot gases. Over millions of years, the surface of the earth cooled and formed the solid crust we

Two canoeists on their way down the Nahanni River in Canada stop to soak in a natural hot spring.

The Story of Fenton Hill

Not every quest is successful. By definition, an experiment carries a risk of failure. If there is no risk, it's not a true experiment. Scientists and engineers do everything they can to maximize the chances of success of an experiment, but they can't guarantee it. Sometimes, they make an error of judgment. Sometimes, they don't have the information they need and their guesses are wrong. There are many reasons why the path of discovery goes backward, and sideways, as well as forward. This is the story of science. It's the story of Fenton Hill.

The concept called hot dry rock was developed in the 1970s at Los Alamos National Laboratory. This was a decade when the price of fossil fuels had gotten very high, and there was a lot of interest in other sources of energy. As luck would have it, a nearby location was suitable for testing the hot dry rock concept. This was Fenton Hill, on the west edge of Valles Caldera, the large volcanic complex in the Jemez Mountains of New Mexico. Beneath Fenton Hill was hard, impermeable crystalline rock, with "dry" heat close to the

In 1921, the first geothermal power plant in the United States opened at The Geysers. It produced enough electricity to light the buildings and streets at the resort. In 1960, construction began of a full-scale, 11-megawatt plant. After this, a number of different companies built power plants in the area. In fact, they overproduced the reservoir, meaning that the pressure of the hot water underground began to decline because so much was being brought to the surface. In the late 1990s, the city of nearby Santa Rosa and other local communities began piping their wastewater to The Geysers and injecting it underground. This helped replace the water and maintain the pressure of the reservoir. Today, there are 21 power plants at The Geysers, producing a total of 750 megawatts of electricity—enough to power a city the size of San Francisco.

Other conventional geothermal resources exist in the United States and elsewhere around the world. The countries of Iceland and the Philippines are among the world's largest producers of geothermal electricity.

The Geysers, in California, was the first geothermal generating plant in the United States. It remains productive today.

Enhanced Geothermal Systems

The number of places with conventional geothermal resources is limited because both water and heat must be present. Many of the good places of this kind have already been developed with power plants. But there are many more places that have heat without water. Tapping into a hotter, dryer, and often deeper geothermal resource is known as *hot dry rock*.

Hot dry rock technology was developed at Los Alamos National Laboratory in the 1970s, and it works like this. First, you choose an area that is known to be very hot at shallow depths. It also requires hard rock that is impermeable, meaning that water doesn't move through it. Next, you drill one hole downward into this hot impermeable rock. After that, you crack the rock underground to make a network of fractures that water can flow through. Then you drill a second downward hole into the fracture network to make a loop. Finally, you pump cold water from the surface into one hole and through the fracture network, where it heats up. You extract it hot from the second hole and use it to power a steam-electric generator. The story of Fenton Hill (see the sidebar) is the story of the first hot dry rock project. Because this project met with only limited success, most potential hot dry rock sites are still waiting to be developed. Right now, they are seen as expensive and with some risk. That's why more research is being done—what if a company invests lots of money and the project fails to deliver? But as the price of fossil fuels rises, hot dry rock systems will be increasingly more competitive.

surface. These are the conditions necessary for constructing a hot dry rock system. The project required geologists (earth scientists) to collaborate with engineers (professionals who design technology). The team first drilled one well 10,000 feet (3,000 meters) deep. At this depth, they found dry rock hotter than 392 degrees F. (200 degrees C.). Water boils at 212 degrees F. (100 degrees C.). So far, so good—they had found hot dry rock.

Next they engineered a fracture system in the rock through a technique called *hydrofraccing* (rhymes with *cracking*). This meant pumping water down the well to produce high pressure that cracked the surrounding rock. Seismic waves—the sound waves produced by the cracking rock—were used to map the fracture network. Scientists were able to translate the sound waves into visual images of the underground fractures. This allowed them to locate and map the fractures without being able to see them directly.

Because of the success of phase 1, the government funded phase 2, which was going to be a bigger, deeper, and hotter system. Phase 2 was drilled to 14,500 feet (4.400

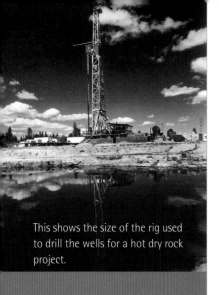

This shows the size of the rig used to drill the wells for a hot dry rock project.

meters) and the temperature was about 617 degrees F. (325 degrees C.).

At this point, the team made a decision that Fraser Goff, who worked for the hot dry rock project at that time, calls a mistake. "The mistake was that they drilled the two holes before they hydrofracced. They felt so confident that they knew which way the fractures would go that they drilled the two holes in advance. They should have drilled the first hole, then done the fraccing, mapped out where the fractures went, and then drilled the second hole to intersect, like they did in phase one." He calls what they should have done "drill crack drill," and what they did do, he calls "drill drill crack." Unfortunately, the cracks went the wrong way, and the team couldn't get the two wells to connect. Goff says, "It's just that simple."

Low-Temperature Systems

A revolutionary new geothermal plant opened at the Chena Hot Springs Resort in Alaska in 2006. This plant produces electricity from low-temperature geothermal water. Chena's water is warm, but nowhere near boiling, and for a long time it was thought that this water wasn't suitable for electricity generation. The typical electrical generating plant, remember, uses steam to turn a turbine, which then runs a generator. Without boiling water, you have no steam, and your turbine doesn't turn. However, new technology has overcome that problem.

The Chena plant brings the pipe of warm water alongside another pipe, which contains a liquid refrigerant called R-134a. As the two pipes travel together, the water transfers its heat to the refrigerant. This is called a heat exchanger. The refrigerant vaporizes at a low temperature—much lower than water's boiling point. So as it absorbs the water's heat, the liquid becomes vapor, expands, and turns the turbine. This system is known as a *binary power plant* because it uses a two-part system to make the turbine turn.

People in Chena are excited because now they can produce electricity to power their whole resort. But outside Chena, there's also excitement about this innovative system. The reason? There are lots of low-temperature geothermal resources in many parts of the world. If you don't need boiling water to produce electricity—if warm water will do—then geothermal's potential goes up dramatically.

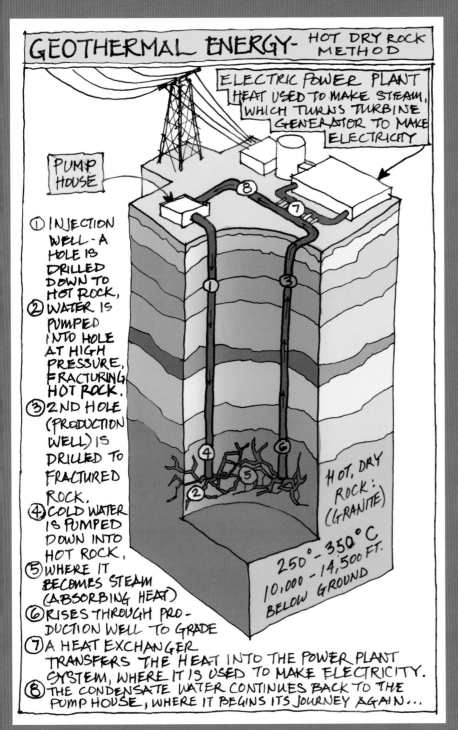

GEOTHERMAL ENERGY- HOT DRY ROCK METHOD

ELECTRIC POWER PLANT HEAT USED TO MAKE STEAM, WHICH TURNS TURBINE GENERATOR TO MAKE ELECTRICITY

PUMP HOUSE

① INJECTION WELL - A HOLE IS DRILLED DOWN TO HOT ROCK,

② WATER IS PUMPED INTO HOLE AT HIGH PRESSURE, FRACTURING HOT ROCK.

③ 2ND HOLE (PRODUCTION WELL) IS DRILLED TO FRACTURED ROCK.

④ COLD WATER IS PUMPED DOWN INTO HOT ROCK,

⑤ WHERE IT BECOMES STEAM (ABSORBING HEAT)

⑥ RISES THROUGH PRODUCTION WELL TO GRADE

⑦ A HEAT EXCHANGER TRANSFERS THE HEAT INTO THE POWER PLANT SYSTEM, WHERE IT IS USED TO MAKE ELECTRICITY.

⑧ THE CONDENSATE WATER CONTINUES BACK TO THE PUMP HOUSE, WHERE IT BEGINS ITS JOURNEY AGAIN...

HOT, DRY ROCK: (GRANITE)

250° - 350°C 10,000 - 14,500 FT. BELOW GROUND

The team spent a lot of money redrilling, and the project got very expensive. Meanwhile, in the 1980s, fossil fuels were getting cheaper and the government was losing interest in geothermal research. The project was finally abandoned in the late 1990s without ever becoming a commercial success.

The project at Fenton Hill wasn't a wasted effort. Phase 1 proved that the hot dry rock concept worked, and the research team learned lots about seismic methods and deep drilling in hot environments. But the project didn't accomplish what it had set out to accomplish. These are common problems with big projects. Uncertainty, human errors, and high costs are the names of the challenges in the quest to power the future.

Ground Source Heat Pumps

Geothermal energy has big promise in another way: it can come from a geothermal or *ground source heat pump.*

Ground source heat pumps use the earth for pre-heating of electrical heat and pre-cooling of air conditioning. They make use of the fact that just a few feet underground, the earth is 56 degrees F. (13 degrees C.) year-round.

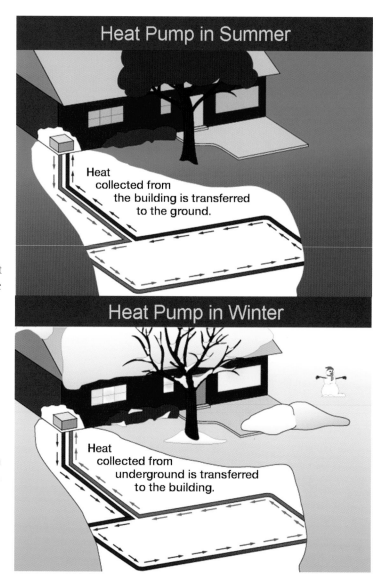

A geothermal heat pump makes use of the constant temperature of the ground a few feet below the surface of the earth, which remains at about 55 degrees F. (13 degrees C.) year-round. In the summer, the heat pump collects heat from the building and discards it underground. In the winter, the process is reversed: the heat pump collects heat from underground and brings it into the building.

Heat pumps can make electrical heating and cooling very efficient. Because they are large, expensive systems, they are good investments for large buildings, like schools or hospitals. Ground source heat pumps don't need to be near a special geothermal resource. In this case, the earth itself is the resource. All over the planet, this technology has potential.

Geothermal in the Future

Roger Hill, an engineer at Sandia National Laboratories, was part of an initiative known as Geopowering the West and has experience with renewable energy. He explains that geothermal plants can operate 24/7. "Geothermal has a high capacity factor. It's not an intermittent resource, the resource is there all the time, so the power plant can operate all the time. It has low emissions because it's not burning any fuels. I think it's going to have a resurgence. It's often mentioned now along with solar and wind as a renewable energy source."

Hill says that the low cost of fossil fuels prevented development of geothermal energy. Why go for something expensive and uncertain when fossil fuels are easily available? But he sees the future differently. "I see much greater increases in prices, especially in fossil fuels, but this all creates opportunities, as the prices rise, for renewables. So I see a future of increasing costs and increasing renewables." How does he advise young people to view geothermal energy? "Just be aware of it, the sleeping beauty, right under our feet."

Spotlight on the Philippines

The Philippines is an island chain of volcanoes, and the country is building more and more geothermal power plants to take advantage of its great geothermal resource. Soon, this small, densely populated country may become the leading producer of geothermal energy worldwide.

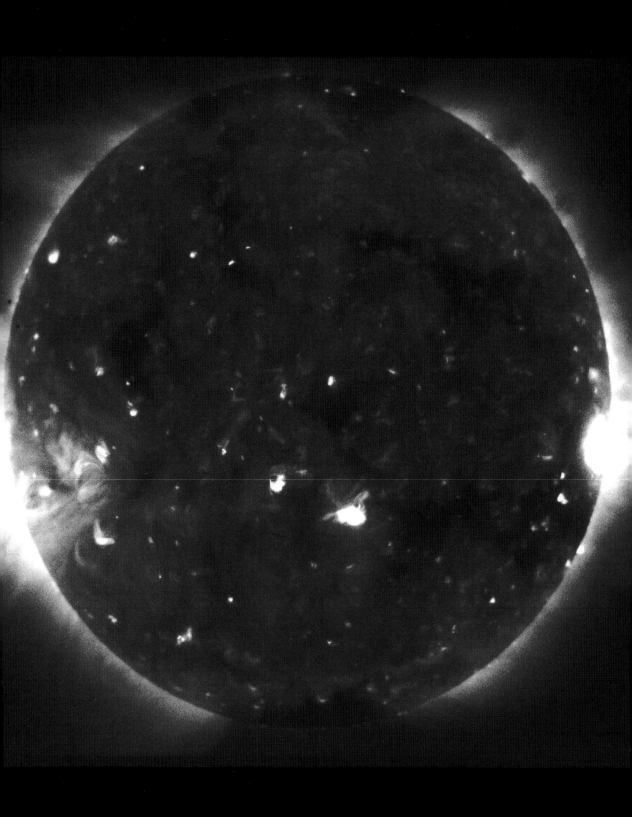

CHAPTER 5

Solar Powered

Where does most energy on earth come from? Now you get to say, "The sun!" and you're right. But you may not realize just how much of life owes its energy to the sun. Almost everything we see and experience around us is made possible by solar energy.

All living things depend on the sun. Plants have the amazing ability to take sunlight and turn it directly into food. This chemical process, which is called *photosynthesis*, uses water, carbon dioxide, and sunlight to produce sugar and oxygen. The plant sucks up water through its roots, gets carbon dioxide and sunlight through its leaves, and uses it all to produce a sugar called glucose in the green cells of its leaves. The plant keeps the sugar and releases oxygen into the air as a by-product. Later, the plant uses the sugar to grow its body. What it doesn't use, the plant stores in the form of chemical energy. This is why people say that sugar is "indirect solar energy"— it stores energy that it got from the sun.

A herbivorous, or plant-eating, animal depends on the indirect solar energy stored in plants. This is another way to say that the animal needs to eat them. Once the plant is eaten, its chemical energy becomes part of the animal's body. The animal uses food energy to move, grow, and stay warm. One day, a carnivorous, or meat-eating, animal may eat the herbivore. Then the herbivore's chemical energy becomes part of the carnivore's body. But it all started with the sunlight that fell on the leaves of a green plant.

From time to time, when a plant or an animal dies in a swamp or in the ocean, its body is buried underground and gradually turns into a fossil. Over millions of years, some of its chemicals are replaced by rock. Other chemicals remain. The carbons that hold chemical energy are still present in the fossil. Coal is almost entirely carbon. Oil and *natural gas* are largely carbon. These fossils are still storing the energy that a green plant originally captured from the sun. This is why fossil fuels are another indirect form of solar energy. When we burn them, we are using energy from the sun that has been stored underground for millions of years.

Even wind is a form of solar energy. When the sun shines on the earth, the side of the globe that is in daylight warms up, but the side in darkness doesn't. Hot air is lighter and less dense than cold air, and it begins to rise. Cold air rushes into the gap left by the rising hot air. Wind is created—one more indirect result of the sun's mighty power.

All this may lead you to another question. If almost everything is solar energy in one way or another, what do we mean when we talk about getting power from "solar energy"?

The answer isn't that hard to understand. When we talk about solar power, we mean energy that comes straight from the sun. It doesn't have to be stored in plants or animals or fossils. You don't have to burn something to get it back. You use sunlight as directly as possible in order to meet your energy needs. People have been doing this for hundreds of thousands of years. On a sunny day in the winter, where do you sit for warmth—in the shade? No—even your dog knows to sleep in the sun! People in cold climates have traditionally designed their houses to open onto the south—which is the direction the sun comes from in the winter. This allows the sun's rays to come through their windows and doors and warm their homes.

The most direct uses of solar energy are called *passive solar techniques*. South-facing windows are a classic example of a passive solar technology. So are solar ovens, which can cook food outside on a sunny day. Solar hot water systems are increasingly popular. These have a rooftop collector that uses the sun's energy to heat water for household use.

This public school building in Northern California has many solar design features. The windows face south for maximum solar exposure. What look like twinkling diamonds in the roof are skylights that bring natural light (called daylighting) into the classrooms. In addition, the roof is covered with photovoltaic panels, which produce electricity for the school.

Photovoltaics, or solar-electric panels, are a more complex solar technology that is becoming more and more widely used. Photovoltaics are flat panels that face south. They sit on rooftops or other places that receive full sun all day long. Through a series of chemical reactions inside the panels, the sunlight that falls on them is converted into electricity. This electricity flows out of the panel through electrical wires. It can either be stored in a battery or sent into the electrical grid.

An *active solar technology* uses a small energy input to collect a larger amount of solar energy. (You can think of this as spending a dime in order to make a dollar.) Concentrating solar power is an active solar technology. It uses a series of mirrors that move to follow the sun. (The movement of the mirrors is what makes it "active" since an input of energy is required to make them move.) The mirrors focus the sun's rays on a single point or area. The concentrated sunlight heats that area to high temperatures, and the heat is used to boil water. The resulting steam is converted into electric power, and the electricity is fed into the grid through wires.

Wind turbines, which use indirect solar energy, are one of the fastest-growing technologies in the world. The turbines turn in the wind and convert the wind's energy into electrical energy, which then flows out of the turbine through wires. Turbines can be small or large, can be built singly or in "farms" of hundreds, and can connect into the electrical grid or stand on their own.

Solar technologies have captured many people's imaginations. They don't pour pollutants into the atmosphere. They don't use expensive fuel—in fact, they use no fuel at all. Their energy source is free and plentiful: sunlight itself. Solar technologies are called clean, renewable technologies—"clean" because they don't pollute and "renewable" because their energy source is never used up.

Concentrating Solar Power

In the year 212 BC, the Romans attacked the Greek city of Syracuse from the sea. Legend has it that the people of Syracuse turned to Archimedes, the great mathematician and inventor, for help. According to the story, Archimedes told all the soldiers to polish their shields till they shone like mirrors. Then he positioned the soldiers along the coast, facing the oncoming Roman ships. When Archimedes gave a signal, the soldiers used their shields to reflect the light of the sun onto the first ship's sails. The sails burst into flame. *Concentrating solar power* (*CSP*) was born.

The basic concepts of solar technology are nothing new. The first concentrating solar power plant was built almost 100 years ago in Egypt, by American inventor Frank Shuman. Shuman chose Egypt because of its sunny climate and the number of wealthy British businessmen who owned land there. He got a large number of these wealthy people excited about his project and willing to pay for it. By 1913, the plant was operating at 55 horsepower—meaning it could do the same work as 55 horses. It was used to pump water, irrigating large tracts of land that had previously been desert. Shuman and his investors were thrilled by the success of the project, and he had plans to build an even larger plant in the Sahara desert. Then World War I began, and everything changed. The world went into war mode, and Shuman's plans were forgotten. After the war, large fields of oil were discovered in various countries. The world turned its attention to fossil fuels and began to produce cheap oil and coal in large quantities. Solar technologies languished. But Shuman's words stay with us: "One thing I feel sure of . . . is that the human race must finally utilize direct sun power or revert to barbarism."

Tom Mancini, at Sandia National Laboratories, works on concentrating solar technologies. There are three different kinds: *parabolic trough*, *power tower*, and *dish Stirling systems*. Mancini explains, "All three of these technologies, even though they're different, do the same thing. You have mirrors oriented in such a way that they reflect sunlight to a region or a point, and you have to efficiently collect that energy. It's collected in a fluid, which gets heated up to a very high temperature, and you use that to generate steam that is used in a standard power cycle to produce electricity. Instead of generating heat from coal and natural gas, which you burn, you're getting heat from solar energy."

CONCENTRATING SOLAR POWER

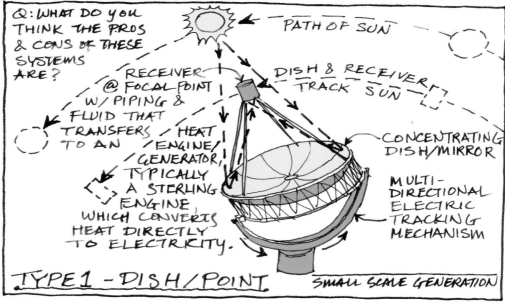

Q: WHAT DO YOU THINK THE PROS & CONS OF THESE SYSTEMS ARE?

PATH OF SUN

RECEIVER @ FOCAL POINT W/ PIPING & FLUID THAT TRANSFERS HEAT TO AN ENGINE/ GENERATOR, TYPICALLY A STERLING ENGINE, WHICH CONVERTS HEAT DIRECTLY TO ELECTRICITY.

DISH & RECEIVER TRACK SUN

CONCENTRATING DISH/MIRROR

MULTI-DIRECTIONAL ELECTRIC TRACKING MECHANISM

TYPE 1 - DISH/POINT   SMALL SCALE GENERATION

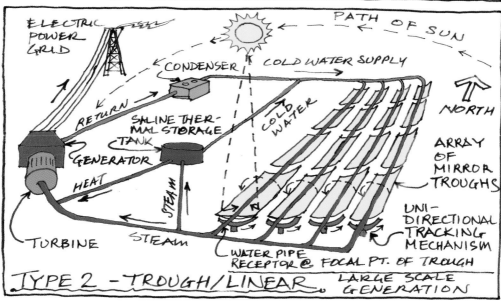

ELECTRIC POWER GRID

PATH OF SUN

CONDENSER   COLD WATER SUPPLY

RETURN

SALINE THER-MAL STORAGE TANK

GENERATOR

HEAT

COLD WATER

NORTH

ARRAY OF MIRROR TROUGHS

UNI-DIRECTIONAL TRACKING MECHANISM

TURBINE   STEAM   STEAM

WATER PIPE RECEPTOR @ FOCAL PT. OF TROUGH

TYPE 2 - TROUGH/LINEAR   LARGE SCALE GENERATION

All forms of concentrating solar power are designed first to convert sunlight to heat energy, then heat energy to mechanical energy, and finally mechanical energy to electricity. All of them have moving parts because as the sun moves, so must the mirrors that reflect its light. These mirrors are known as *heliostats*, a word that comes from the ancient Greek roots that mean "making the sun stand." Mancini explains, "If you think about how a heliostat tracks, if it's going to reflect the light of the sun to a fixed point, it's going to have to be moving over the course of the day."

Mancini describes what kind of work is going on today to improve these time-honored technologies and make them less expensive. "There's a lot of research and development going on in materials, engineering design, and new fluids to increase performance and reduce cost. You can't schedule breakthroughs, but you have ideas, and you pursue them, and you're not sure where they're going to take you. We think the window for concentrating solar is opening wide right now." Mancini says, "We're big power. We're not talking about little solar generators; we're talking about big, utility-scale power systems." By "utility scale" he means that concentrating solar power plants are meant to compete with coal-burning plants, which currently give us about 55 percent of our electricity. Utilities are the companies that buy and sell big power and deliver it to our communities.

This solar trough is one form of concentrating solar power, also known as solar thermal power. The curved mirror reflects the sun's light onto a fluid that flows through the central tubing. The fluid heats up, becomes steam, and turns a turbine to create electricity.

One of the disadvantages of solar power is that it's only produced when the sun shines. In the evening, as people come home and turn on their lights and TVs and computers, sunlight is on the wane. But what if you could collect extra solar power during the day and store it until evening? Mancini says that one advantage of concentrating solar power is its potential for what is called *thermal storage*. Other renewable technologies, like wind turbines and photovoltaics, don't have

Photovoltaics

Photovoltaic (PV) panels are flat semiconductor sheets specially designed to take the light of the sun and convert it directly to electricity. They are shiny and eye catching, coming in colors like dark gray or deep blue that sparkle in the sun. They are also expensive, and Charles Hanley is working on that. Hanley, and his team at Sandia National Laboratories, are working to make the panels last longer, produce more electricity, and cost less. He explains, "The big objective here is that by 2015 or so, PV systems will cost much the same as other generation technologies, like coal, oil, and natural gas. Now, that's a big goal, but it's what we're working toward. If we reach it, PV will just take off."

Hanley and his team spend their time in front of computers, in laboratories, on the phone, and at meetings. They write computer programs that model what advanced PV systems will do and collect data in the lab that test these computer models. Science can involve

Photovoltaic panels generate electricity without creating steam or turning a turbine. They are modular and can easily fit on rooftops that are sunny and south facing.

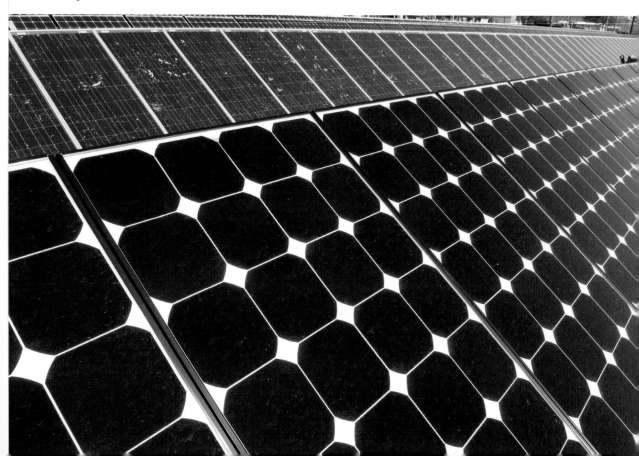

working with things that are small, but Hanley explains that what his team is really thinking about is something huge. It's what Hanley calls "the next version of our U.S. energy infrastructure," meaning the way our country will get and use energy in the future. Hanley pictures "a global electric grid that uses local resources like solar, like wind, like geothermal, and where you don't have these gigantic power plants, with these huge smokestacks, in the Four Corners [where the states of Colorado, Utah, Arizona, and New Mexico touch] or elsewhere. You'll have smaller versions and only where needed. Electric power will be much more locally oriented, and it will be nearly pollution free, and it will be extremely reliable."

Cost has been the main reason why solar systems aren't more widely available. In 2007, it's not difficult to provide an average American home with photovoltaic panels that will produce as much electricity as the home consumes—especially in the sunny desert. But these PV panels may cost over $20,000. An average household's electric consumption costs only several hundred dollars a year. You can see why people are reluctant to invest in PV. Even though the system may sit on their roof for 30 years providing them with clean and free electricity, it will take decades before their savings make up for the cost of the initial investment.

What kinds of improvements will make PV panels less expensive? A couple of things, says Hanley. One is simplifying the manufacturing process. This might mean cutting down on the number of steps needed to make a panel. Another is reducing the need for expensive materials. Most PV panels depend on silicon crystals to capture the light of the sun. Silicon is fairly pricey, and the large quantity needed increases the cost of the panels. If engineers can develop what Hanley calls "thinner wafers," the panels will need less silicon and cost less.

One of the advantages of PV systems is that they can either be *grid tied* or *self-contained*. A grid-tied system is wired into the electric mineral deposits and quickly become useless? She reveals that the manufacturers tell people NOT to use tap water in this system. They say the minerals in tap water will clog up the system and advise that only purified water be used or another fluid like antifreeze, which is contained in a tube or pipe that crosses paths with the water pipe, sending its heat across the barrier (this is called a heat exchanger). But this would make the system more complicated, and the goal at Zomeworks is always to simplify. So Beauchamp wants to see what will happen if she breaks the rules and passes tap water directly through the collector. Will it work? Will it bust? Will it clog? These are the questions driving her research.

Another Zomeworks system works along the same lines as the solar hot water tank, but it heats space instead of water. This is a big radiator made of plastic piping that is full of hot water from the roof. There is one downstairs, but it's not on during this tour, although it's chilly outside. Someone explains, "We turned it off. It was getting too hot."

Once more on the roof, Beauchamp shows a third Zomeworks invention—the sunbender. This is a curved piece of metal that reflects sunlight down into a skylight. It makes the skylights more efficient by filling them with extra light. The sunbenders on the roof of Zomeworks direct light into the factory below, where employees make the products that Zomeworks sells. Beauchamp says, "The sunbenders are another example of Steve's innovation. You bring more natural light into a space. You're keeping people connected to the natural world and to the seasons. Our guys in the shop are in there all year, from six in the morning till four. Being connected to the outdoors is good for your well-being. You know, we are all animals."

Beauchamp is an Albuquerque native. She graduated from La Cueva High School, then got a college degree and a master's degree in environmental science. "I really got interested in using our natural resources, which are very abundant, to try to figure out how we can live with our resources, our environment, in a way that isn't harmful. So to me energy is a huge issue." She is optimistic that her generation can tackle this huge issue. "I'm 25. People my age and younger—we've grown up in a world where environmental concerns are something we've always lived with. Whereas for people of my parents' generation and my grandparents' generation, environmental concerns were never really at the forefront. So we young people have a vision of the world, and a vision of how we have to live in the world, that is fundamentally different. And that's why I'm hopeful that we can really use what people of past generations have learned about passive energy, renewable energy, but also take it to a different level, to where it really does become mainstream."

Helene Beauchamp shows a solar thermal hot water system on the roof of Zomeworks.

Spotlight on Spain

This sunny country is rapidly investing in several forms of solar power—photovoltaic, concentrating solar power, and wind. Spanish companies are taking the lead worldwide in the revival of concentrating solar power. And the country will soon be home to a 20-megawatt photovoltaic plant, the biggest in the world.

Spotlight on Germany

Germany is the world's largest user of wind energy. This cloudy country is also the biggest producer of photovoltaic power and is using increasing amounts of it. A 2001 German law mandates the gradual elimination of nuclear power. Germany is betting on a renewable energy future.

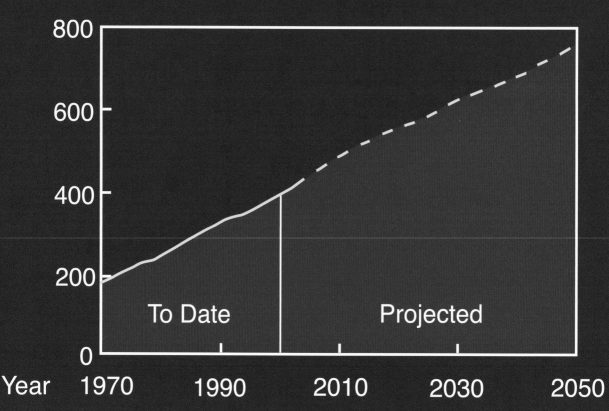

Worldwide Energy Use
(Quadrillion Btu)

800

600

400

200

0

To Date

Projected

Year   1970   1990   2010   2030   2050

How much energy will the world use 30 years from now? Forecasts predict huge increases in energy consumption as the world's population rises and increases its standard of living. A British thermal unit (Btu) is the amount of heat required to raise the temperature of one pound of water one degree Fahrenheit.

CHAPTER 6
Reducing Our Use

The world's population continues to grow, and our energy use is growing even faster than our population. The Energy Information Agency (EIA), which is a branch of the U.S. government, predicts that worldwide *energy consumption* will increase 57 percent from 2004 to 2030. That means that by the time today's young people are adults, the world will be using about one and a half times the energy it uses today. That's a huge jump in consumption.

In developing its *forecast*, the EIA made the assumption that "current laws and policies remain unchanged" until 2030. That assumption is commonly known as "business as usual." When people develop a "business as usual" forecast, they want to predict what will happen if people keep behaving the way they are behaving now. Currently, the people of the world consume considerably more energy every year than we did the previous year. The EIA's forecast assumes this behavior will continue.

But what if it doesn't?

The fastest way to address our energy problem is to reduce our use. Providing new energy takes time. New wind and solar power plants take several years to build. Geothermal and nuclear plants may take decades. But if we use less energy, we help solve the problem immediately. There are two main ways to use less. One is *energy conservation*: saving energy. The other is *energy efficiency*: using smarter machines.

Energy Conservation

Saving energy requires changes in behavior. This can be as simple as remembering to turn off the lights when you leave a room. It can be as high tech as installing a timer on the family thermostat that will turn it down in the middle of the night. Saving energy includes walking instead of driving and putting on a sweater instead of turning up the heat. What other examples can you think of from your own life?

Every choice to conserve is small in its own right, but together they add up. This can be observed in big differences between nations in per-person energy use. In Japan, for example, the average person uses less than half of the energy used by an average American, even though Japan is a wealthy, developed country like the United States. Why such a difference? The reasons are cultural and economic. In Japan, energy has always been expensive and citizens have been encouraged to pay attention to how they use it. In the United States, energy has been cheap for a long time and people have used it freely. Now that energy costs are rising across the world, everybody is beginning to pay attention to energy use. Americans may find there are many simple things that will help them conserve in their homes and businesses.

Energy Efficiency

Efficiency means doing the same work with less waste. This is why we call efficient technologies "smarter." Some efficient technologies are brand new, and some are old as the hills. But they have one thing in common: they use less energy.

You may recall from chapter 1 that the three main areas in which people use energy are buildings, transportation, and food. Let's now look at each of these *sectors* in turn and consider how they could be made smarter and more energy efficient.

———————

This Japanese home features many energy-efficient and renewable energy design features. Look closely and you will see (1) a solar-thermal hot water system on the upper left of the roof, (2) photovoltaic panels on the right side of the roof, (3) many south-facing windows to maximize solar gain, and (4) solar drying of food and laundry on the patio.

BUILDINGS

In a single word, Ed Mazria explains the way to create smarter buildings. That word is *design*. What is he talking about?

Mazria is an architect in Santa Fe. He has designed some of New Mexico's urban landmarks, like the conservatory in the Albuquerque Biopark, where tropical plants grow, and the Genoveva Chavez Community Center in Santa Fe, where hundreds of families go to swim, ice-skate, and have fun. He is also a man with a mission. That mission: to stop global warming by changing the way we build. He's a tall man with a big mustache, a firm voice, and a strong sense of hope and optimism.

The way Mazria tells it, a hundred years ago, people knew how to build for energy efficiency. They used thick walls that would keep their structures warm in the winter and cool in the summer. They planned windows in a way that would move air through the buildings in the summer. Energy was precious, and people were careful not to waste it. This was true for homes, businesses, and public buildings. Then something changed. That something was the world of fossil fuels.

Fossil fuels had been around for a while already, but in the first half of the 20th century, they really took off. Huge oil and gas reserves began to be tapped. The price of these fuels dropped. Architects took note, and they began to change the way they did buildings.

This was the era of the skyscrapers. Big steel frames allowed buildings to shoot up higher than they had ever risen before. Instead of thick walls, these buildings needed to have lightweight, thin walls. Instead of windows that opened (you don't want to fall from the 40th floor!), these buildings had large picture windows that were fixed in place. The solution for heating and cooling these giants? Never fear, said the architects: this is the age of cheap fossil fuels. We can make your building like a world of its own—almost like a spaceship sealed off from its surroundings. If you're cold, you just turn up the heat. If you're hot, you put on the air conditioning.

Smaller buildings followed the example of the skyscrapers. Large windows became the fashion. Their single panes let in cold air during the winter, but that wasn't considered a problem in the age of cheap fossil fuels. Walls were built thinner, which saved money. They transmitted cold air in the winter and heat in the summer, but again, that wasn't considered a problem. It was cheaper to heat and cool a home than to build it with solid materials. Few people knew about global warming yet or worried about the time when the fuels might run low.

This kind of building design has continued up until today, when many of our structures are still built as if energy is cheap and causes no problems. But the reality, says Mazria, has changed—and architecture needs to change along with it. We now know that fossil fuels have a great cost. Not only our pocketbook but also our environment is at risk. We have to redesign buildings to reflect this new reality.

And Mazria is hopeful that we can do it. "Here's how we're going to turn this thing around," he says. The good news is that the elements of good design are already known, and they aren't hard to put into practice. Face your buildings south to let in the heat and light of the winter sun. Shade those south-facing windows in the summer. Invest in good insulation for your walls, windows, and roof to keep out the cold and the heat. Plan your windows in a way that lights your rooms with sunlight and allows breezes through in the summer. If you do sensible things like these, he says, you can reduce energy use in new buildings by half—easily and immediately.

These energy-efficient homes include features like walls made of recycled tires, large banks of south-facing windows, and north-facing walls built into a hillside for natural insulation from heat and cold.

But half, 50 percent, isn't enough. In order to protect our climate, Mazria's organization Architecture 2030 calls for buildings to be completely carbon neutral by the year 2030. This means we must eliminate their fossil fuel use by that time: we must cut it 100 percent. Where else can we find ways to save energy? Let's look at what goes on inside a building.

There are four main energy hogs in buildings: heating, cooling, hot water, and lighting. Proper design can cut the need for heating, cooling, and lighting in half. But there will still be a demand for electric lights, some heat, some air conditioning, refrigeration, and hot water. These technologies can all be improved and made more efficient.

A better furnace is a simple way to make heating more efficient. A furnace burns the fuel that produces heat for a building. New furnaces are much more efficient than they used to be. As an alternative to furnaces, high-tech ways to produce efficient heat include the *air-source heat pump* and the ground-source heat pump. Heat pumps use electricity, but they are much more efficient than traditional plug-in space heaters, which are the very worst way to warm up a room. The ground source pumps, which were mentioned in chapter 4, use the constant temperature below the earth's surface to pre-heat buildings.

There are also lower-tech ways to heat buildings. *Solar homes* are set up to take advantage of the sun's energy both day and night. Water and brick are two materials that have high thermal mass, meaning they store lots of heat. If a big tank of water or a big brick wall is built just inside large south-facing windows, the water and the brick will warm up in the sun all day and release heat all night. More complex solar heating can include water pipes that run into a room or under its floor. Solar systems can also heat or pre-heat tap water. Systems like these at Zomeworks are featured in chapter 5.

For cooling, better air conditioners are being designed. This is important because the typical *refrigerated air* technology is one of our biggest energy users. In dry parts of the country, a technology called the *evaporative cooler* is a more efficient alternative. This is also known as the *swamp cooler* because it uses water for the cooling. Although it uses more water than refrigerated air does, a swamp cooler uses less energy. In humid parts of the country, though, the swamp cooler isn't effective. It only makes sense in a place where water evaporates quickly.

The household appliance that typically uses the most energy year-round is the refrigerator. Some fridges are more efficient than others. Our federal government has a label called *Energy Star* on efficient appliances to help consumers make choices about what to buy. If people learn to look for the Energy Star label when they shop for big appliances like fridges, clothes washers and dryers, furnaces, and water heaters, they can make choices that will save them energy and money over the long run.

Large appliances last awhile, and people don't have to replace them very often. But in the area of lighting, people are always replacing a small piece of technology. That is, of course, the lightbulb.

Our traditional technology, the *incandescent bulb*, produces light by glowing white-hot. It's an inefficient technology because most of the electricity needed to power it goes into producing heat, not light. Touch one of these bulbs when it's been on, and you'll burn your hand.

The modern bulb called the *compact fluorescent light* (*CFL*) works differently. Special gases inside a long glass tube fluoresce, or light up, when they encounter an electric current. Fluorescent bulbs get warm but not hot. They use only one-quarter the electricity needed by an incandescent of similar brightness. Compact fluorescents are a more efficient lightbulb, saving energy and money as they do their job.

Compact fluorescent lights aren't perfect. They contain a little mercury, which is a hazardous substance. When they break or burn out, these bulbs shouldn't go into the regular landfill. They need to be recycled or treated as hazardous waste. But advocates of energy efficiency point out that coal-burning power plants also produce mercury. In fact, they spew it into the air we breathe. If you use CFLs, you're reducing the need for coal-generated electricity, which causes carbon dioxide pollution as well as mercury pollution.

A more recent technology promises even greater energy savings in lighting. This is the *light-emitting diode* (*LED*), also known as solid-state lighting. Light-emitting diodes don't use hazardous substances, consume very little energy to do their job, and last for years. Their main disadvantage now is cost. Scientists and engineers are working to bring down the cost of this new technology. Believe it or not, a lot of the cost of an LED is the fault of the color green.

White light is a mixture of different wavelengths—blue, red, and green all combined. LEDs can produce strong wavelengths of blue and red, but their green is much dimmer. This makes white LED light expensive—it has to use enough power to produce a strong green for the mix. Jerry Simmons, a scientist at Sandia National Laboratories, is working on green. He told the Albuquerque *Tribune* newspaper, "Green is considered by many to be the most important challenge in solid state lighting . . . We think in 10 years, especially if we can solve this problem, LED lights will be more than twice as efficient as compact fluorescents."

In the meantime, LEDs are cost-effective in some settings already. If you need a little night-light, flashlight, or closet light, an LED is the way to go. They also make sense for lights that are always on. Cities around the country have been saving hundreds of thousands of dollars by replacing their traffic lights with LEDs.

Three kinds of lightbulbs: the traditional incandescent on the left, the compact fluorescent in the center, and the LED on the right. The incandescent and compact fluorescent can light a whole room. The LED is a night-light.

With efficient design and efficient appliances, we could reduce our energy use in buildings a great deal. But we couldn't bring it down to zero. When Ed Mazria talks about "carbon-neutral" buildings, he means efficient buildings that also rely on a clean source of energy to provide the electricity coming into the wall sockets. Now that you have read this far, can you imagine what kind of source or sources those might be?

TRANSPORTATION

Most of our transportation today runs on petroleum products. These include gasoline, diesel, and airplane fuel. Although gasoline is known as "gas" for short, petroleum products are actually all liquid fuels, made from the fossils of tiny marine animals that were buried under ocean sands millions of years ago and squeezed and compressed over the years until they turned into a thick oily goo.

The *internal combustion engine*, which makes an automobile run, was designed after this liquid fuel was discovered about 100 years

This tiny, energy-efficient car was on display at a trade show in Japan. Could cars this small become popular in the United States?

and shopping. But mass transportation is more energy efficient than a fleet of cars and trucks with only one or two people in each of them. A movement has begun in many urban areas to bring back streetcars and light rail and improve city bus systems. A nation-wide effort has not yet been made to restore a good long-distance network of railroads—which would be very hard to do. But it's something to consider. How important do you think this might be to your future?

FOOD

Take a minute tonight to look at the food on your dinner plate and ask yourself where it came from. Yes, it probably came from the store. But before that? And before that? What was the beginning of the story that is going to end in your stomach?

It's been estimated that the average piece of food travels 1,500 miles (2,400 kilometers) to get to you. That's halfway across the United States. Food travels by boat, train, and truck. As we know, transportation takes energy.

Transportation isn't the only energy cost of producing food—far from it. Agriculture in the United States generally uses large amounts of pesticides, herbicides, and *fertilizers*. These products, which kill pests and weeds and make the plants grow strong, are energy intensive to make, and many also contain petroleum. Then there is the machinery used to prepare fields, water them, and harvest crops, which requires lots of fossil fuels. Finally, the processing plants where food is prepared and packaged are big energy users. All of these added together make the food industry our third-biggest consumer of energy, after buildings and transportation.

Because food gives us the energy we need to live, we are naturally willing to put energy into producing it. But we need to ask ourselves

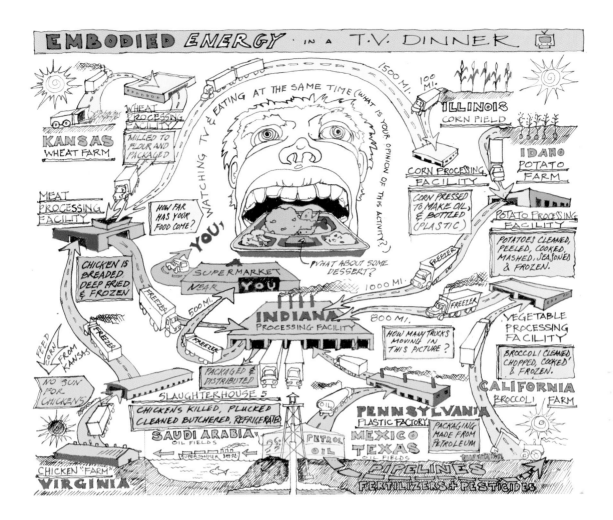

the same efficiency questions we asked for buildings and transportation. How is our current system wasteful? Can we get food in ways that are smarter and more energy efficient?

The quest for efficiency is nothing new. People are always looking for ways to produce more product at a lower cost. A hundred years ago, the biggest cost of agriculture was the labor of the people who worked the land. Efficiency of that labor has improved dramatically. In 1930, one U.S. farmer supplied 10 people with food. By 1970, one farmer supplied 76 people.

How do you think this dramatic increase in food production came about? You're right if once again, you're suspecting a role for fossil fuels. Before the 1800s, human arms and backs supplied the energy that powered U.S. agriculture. In the 1800s, horsepower came to replace human power, and in the 1900s, petroleum-fueled machinery replaced horsepower. In 1954, for the first time, more tractors than horses were working on farms.

The production of cheap nitrogen fertilizers was the other key development in our 20th-century agriculture. By 1970, an average of 32 million tons of commercial fertilizer was spread on fields every year—up from two million tons in 1900. The fertilizer increased *yields,* causing a piece of land to produce much more food than it did before. Because of efficiencies of labor and efficiencies of yield, the cost of food dropped. In 1929, Americans spent 24 percent of their income on food—almost one-quarter of what they earned. Today, they spend only 9 percent.

Some patterns are visible in this story. One is increasing *mechanization.* What people used to do by hand, now machines do for them. Human energy has been replaced by the energy from fossil fuels. Another is *centralization.* A countryside of many small farms, run by families with small equipment, has been transformed into a landscape of mega-farms, huge operations that save money by using big equipment and employing fewer people. These farms depend on big inputs of water and chemicals in order to yield large amounts of low-cost products.

These patterns, while saving the consumer money, have also created some lasting problems. The increased water use has lowered the water table and led to erosion of good soil, which ends up carried away in rivers. Agricultural chemicals have polluted waterways and poisoned helpful insects. Thousands of small farmers have lost their jobs and way of life. Perhaps most troubling, we have become dependent on a system of agriculture that requires huge inputs of fossil fuel energy.

Some people have begun looking for alternatives to this system. *Organic* food has become more popular in our country. On organic farms, crops are grown without the use of chemical fertilizers, pesticides, or herbicides. Many people are willing to pay more for organic products because they believe they are better for their health and better for the environment.

A *local food movement* is also under way. The slogan "buy local" reminds people to notice where their food comes from. Do you want grapes in the winter? They will probably be coming from South America, a voyage of over 4,000 miles (6,440 kilometers). Would you be okay with an apple instead? Many parts of the United States grow apples, and they can be stored all winter. Or perhaps your part of the country grows oranges and grapefruits. The local food movement encourages consumers to learn what food is produced in their area and buy more of that and less of things that have to travel huge distances.

Tom Seibel, a farmer who used to own an organic wheat farm, now lives in Santa Fe. His entire backyard is devoted to a vegetable garden. A hundred years ago, most people had a kitchen garden like this one. Today, it's rare, especially in American cities, to see people growing their own food. But Seibel thinks this is likely to change.

Seibel explains that in other parts of the

Tom Seibel, who used to own a wheat farm in northern New Mexico, now grows wheat in his own backyard in Santa Fe, along with a variety of other food crops.

world, urban agriculture is still flourishing. In the huge Chinese city of Shanghai, for example, about 90 percent of the food is grown within or near the city limits. "My wife is from southern China, a city of a couple million, and they don't have refrigeration. There's a market within walking distance, and they go for almost every meal to the market for fresh meat, vegetables, and fruit. It's so fresh that there's no need for refrigeration. They slaughter chickens and bring them in on the back of their motorcycles from just a few miles away. That's how they feed everybody." He pictures that in the future, food production in our country will look like the rest of the world's, where "production is more localized, like in China with all these little plots—big apartment buildings and then a little space that people are farming." In Seibel's own backyard, he gardens year-round. "The goal is to have something fresh to eat from the garden every day of the year, even in winter."

Don Bustos, a farmer in northern New Mexico, grows many of his vegetables in greenhouses. He uses a solar thermal system to heat one of his greenhouses in the winter.

It was hard for Seibel to make a living as an organic wheat farmer. "You have to buy huge equipment that costs thousands and thousands of dollars, and then the maintenance on it, and the fuel for it, and all the replacement parts, it's expensive." And the land itself is expensive: if you own it, you are either paying a mortgage, or paying property taxes, or both. He has hope for a new kind of farming, where people use small plots—backyards, their friends' backyards, public land—and farm them intensively, without big expensive machines. "If you're talking about backyards and small scale, the biggest expense is the rototiller [the machine that turns the earth over], and you take advantage of family and friends, and get someone to work for you in exchange for produce." He predicts that this way, small farmers can earn a living wage again.

Organic food can be expensive. Will it become affordable for all people, not just the rich? Seibel says that today's situation is the total reverse of how things should be. "The petroleum companies, the chemical companies that make fertilizers and insecticides, and the ones using these things that are endangering the environment and people's health, *they* should be the ones paying extra, and organic should be mainstream. If you want to have these perfect-looking fruits, you should pay a premium for THAT. It's going to be an interesting near future as petroleum gets more and more expensive, because that's what all the fertilizer is made of. Meanwhile, there's a tremendous amount of waste; people bag up all their leaves and take them to the dump. I have a friend who's a landscaper, he brings me all his leaves in the fall, and I make compost out of them." Compost is what Seibel uses to fertilize his organic garden. It's a mixture of broken-down waste products from plants. He says, "If you had a lot of people growing things—I'm not talking everybody has to do this, but if you had 10 percent, even—you would use a lot of these resources that are now going to waste."

Don Bustos, another New Mexico farmer, is testing a solar-heating system in one of his greenhouses near Española. Before the system went in, he had been trying to grow some bedding plants in a cold frame in the greenhouse, and the natural gas bill for one month of heat in the winter was $700. He got a grant to put in a $10,000 solar system. It consists of five solar collectors aboveground, a heat exchanger that transfers the solar-generated heat into a big

CHAPTER 7

Weird Fuels on the Way—Or, Can You Power a Pickup with Pond Scum?

So far, this book has focused on ways to generate electricity, because electrical energy is the form of energy we consume the most of. Everything that plugs into a wall socket runs on electricity. Refrigerators, air conditioners, computers, lights . . . they all depend on what we fondly call "juice." As electric vehicles are developed and marketed, we can picture that soon even our transportation will be mostly plug in.

But even if the cars of the future no longer need gas tanks, we can be pretty sure that some other machines will still need to burn fuel. Big trucks, bulldozers, tractors, airplanes, and industrial machines— these large pieces of equipment will run on petroleum or something similar for the foreseeable future. And petroleum, as a fuel option, is looking worse and worse. As we have seen, it causes pollution and global warming. What's more, it's in short supply and getting increasingly expensive. For Americans, this supply is especially problematic. We use more petroleum than any nation on earth, and at one time we

Opposite: Big machinery and the trucking industry will need to run on liquid fuels for the foreseeable future. Biodiesel may become a practical alternative to fossil fuels—if some problems can first be solved.

salts from the Permian Basin—we're actually making up salt water out of fresh water. We want to use the same water that may be used in the commercial-scale ponds so we understand how the algae reacts to the micronutrients in the water."

This project now is small scale, but if it goes well, it has big potential. Stroud says, "We have top environmental conditions and natural resources in this area: not only the salt water, but the climate—most of the year is sunny and warm. We also have a lot of flat desert land that is available. It could become an enormous industry."

Many people are interested in algae these days. Stroud explains what is different about the Carlsbad project. "There are a variety of different technologies that are being tried, and a lot of them are very complicated and very expensive. Our approach has been to ask: How can we do this in the simplest-possible way?" The goal is to produce oil that costs the same as petroleum or less. She explains how they work on every part of the process. "We may find that it costs X amount to harvest algae and X amount to extract oil from it. If we find that these amounts make the oil cost too much, we have to go back and look for ways to improve the processes so the costs stay low. We have to adjust as we go along. And that's part of the research."

Research can involve a lot of little details, but Stroud talks easily about the big issues. "Diesel consumption in the United States right now is about 60 billion gallons [227 billion liters] per year. When you think about fuel, you probably think about gasoline, like you put in your car. But diesel is really what powers industry. Farm equipment. Eighteen-wheeler trucks—the whole trucking industry. Shipping. To be able to replace diesel with something that is renewable, reliable, and that we can produce within our own United States would be a major accomplishment, and it's really exciting to think about how we can do that." She even makes a connection with the management of hazardous materials, which is what her organization was originally formed to do. "Diesel fuel is causing great amounts of carbon dioxide and particulates [smog] in our air every single day. Biodiesel from algae would be a more environmentally sound way to fuel our industry. That's the connection."

And the virtual tour of the algae farm ends on a personal note. Wren Stroud isn't a scientist. She majored in English in college. "You can do all kinds of interesting jobs with an English degree. A research project requires the ideas and knowledge of many scientists, but the project will also need someone skilled in communications to tell the world what they are doing. Whether students are interested in math and science or language and communications, a lot of good jobs may be on the horizon in the emerging field of algae biodiesel."

Spotlight on Brazil

Brazil has been producing bio-ethanol from sugarcane for over 30 years. This large tropical country is now the world biggest bioethanol producer. All Brazilian fueling stations are required to sell a gasoline-bio-ethanol blend—unless they sell pure bioethanol, which 15 percent of Brazil's cars can run on.

CHAPTER 8

Into the Future

Energy will be a major topic of the 21st century. It may be *the* major topic. Over your lifetime, you can expect to see it playing a bigger and bigger role in political decisions and personal choices. Energy powers our economy, our homes, and our very lives. It's everywhere and touches everything.

This book has described how the age of fossil fuels is drawing to a close. It has told the story of many promising energy alternatives. Which of them will come to dominate the human world? That story is yet to be told.

Many people hope for a miracle cure to our energy problems. They are waiting to hear about a source that will be as cheap and easy to produce as fossil fuels have been. The reality is more complicated. There will probably be no single energy source that will quickly replace coal and oil. We are likely to move to an energy economy that draws from a mix of sources. The sources we have looked at in these pages—nuclear, solar, wind, geothermal, and biofuel—may all be part of the mix. Conservation and efficiency will also be part of the mix.

Recently, there has been a lot of talk about hydrogen. Some people have called it the clean, renewable fuel we have been waiting for. In all the excitement, people missed one important point. Hydrogen gas isn't naturally found on earth. To get large amounts of hydrogen fuel, you must make it from water. This takes energy. Hydrogen is a promising fuel, but other energy sources will be needed to create it. These could be non-renewable sources like coal and nuclear, or renewables like solar and wind, or some combination of these. Moving to the *hydrogen economy* that politicians talk about will not by itself solve the energy problem.

Another big solution that many people are betting on goes by the big name of *carbon capture and sequestration*. This means taking carbon dioxide out of the air and putting it somewhere safe. There is a lot of interest in this approach because it would mean that we could keep on burning coal, which is still plentiful and cheap, although it's the worst producer of carbon dioxide.

The simplest way to take carbon dioxide out of the air is to plant more trees. Unfortunately, around the world we are losing forests instead of gaining them. And even if we were able to turn the entire world into a forest, it wouldn't solve our carbon dioxide problem. So scientists are looking for higher-tech methods of carbon capture and sequestration. These include injecting the gas underground or into the deep ocean.

Daniel Schrag, director of the Harvard University Center for the Environment, thinks the ocean floor will be the best storage spot for carbon dioxide. Picture coal plants that capture carbon dioxide instead of releasing it into the air. Then picture that CO_2 traveling by ocean tanker into the middle of the ocean, where it's pumped down a long tube and buried under ocean sands. Schrag says that thousands of years' worth of carbon dioxide pollution could be stored in the ocean. He believes that this kind of carbon sequestration will be necessary to prevent the worst effects of global warming.

Others are studying the potential of putting the CO_2 into underground cracks, reservoirs, or rocks. Abandoned oil and gas fields are one obvious place to store carbon dioxide since they are empty underground reservoirs. A different project, now under way in Washington

State, is testing the possibility of storing CO_2 underground in lava, which can react with the gas and turn it into a solid called calcium carbonate. This is the same chalky stuff that seashells are made of. There would be an advantage to turning the gas into a solid: that way, it couldn't leak back out into the atmosphere. The problem with storing gases is that they don't always stay where you put them.

Why is it so hard to find a single solution to our energy problem? The answer has to do with issues of scale. Many of the technologies we have looked at are realistic on a small scale but challenging on a big scale. Picture thousands of tons of carbon dioxide being injected into the ocean. Will it change the ocean environment? Will it stay where it's put, or will it come back up to the surface? Picture thousands of nuclear power plants, each producing many tons of radioactive waste. Could we keep all of those plants safe and secure? Could we dispose of all that waste? Picture a solar array the size of Indiana.

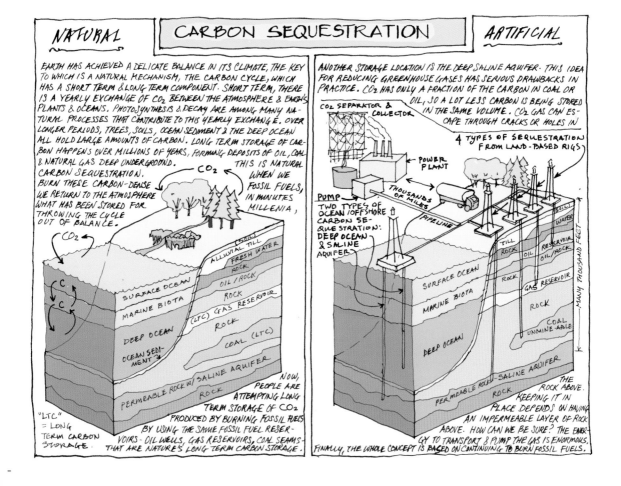

Do we want something that big? Do we have the raw materials to build it? All these questions remain unanswered. This is why a mix of energy technologies is a more likely scenario than a single, dominant mega-technology.

In the meantime, all the technologies and approaches you have read about are competing in the race to replace fossil fuels. Again and again, we have seen that cost is the major obstacle. Coal and petroleum are dirty, but they have been very cheap for a long time. They are getting more expensive, but they are still cheaper than most alternatives. In order to compete, the alternatives must get more cost-effective. Many alternative-energy advocates are looking forward to the day when carbon dioxide has a cost. As this book is written in 2009, power plants can still release as much CO_2 as they wish and pay no price for it. More and more people believe that this situation will change soon—that companies will have to pay to pollute. This will raise the cost of their power. If the cost of fossil fuels goes up, the alternatives will immediately become more cost-effective. In 2009, the president of the United States, Barack Obama, talked about the importance of a *cap and trade* system that will put a cost on carbon emissions.

The race to power the future is full of excitement, challenge, and high energy. We have seen how much exciting research is going on. Energy is a growing field and will create many jobs. There will be jobs for scientists and engineers with advanced degrees, but that's not all. There will also be the need for technicians to build, install, and maintain the equipment. There will be a need for businesspeople who will manage the companies and the products. There will be a need for professional communicators to promote these products to the public. If you have an interest in one of these areas, the field of energy may hold the right career for you.

Let's end where we began, with some words from Wren Stroud, a professional communicator. "I think kids get the idea that science jobs are boring and you're going to hang around and be a lab rat and look at test tubes all day. It's not that. It's very much a 'hmm, let's try this, oops, it didn't work, let's try that' sort of process. It's very creative, and it's exciting and it's fun."

If You Want to Know More about Powering the Future . . .

National Center for Atmospheric Research
www.eo.ucar.edu/kids/green/index.htm
Kids' Crossing: "Living in the Greenhouse"—a site for students to learn about climate and climate change

U.S. Environmental Protection Agency
www.epa.gov/climatechange/kids/index.html
Interactive website for kids on climate
"The Climate Detectives"—scientific evidence about climate change
"What Is the Climate System?" has an animated lesson on the carbon cycle

Climate Change Education.org
www.epa.gov/climatechange/kids/index.html
A website from California with information and curriculum
"The Case of the Warming Planet"—scientific evidence about climate change

Time Magazine special report on global warming April 4, 2006,
www.time.com/time/covers/0,16641,20060403,00.html
Time Magazine photoessay on evidence about global warming,
www.time.com/time/photoessays/2006/global_warming/

National Geographic "Fast Facts on Global Warming"
www.news.nationalgeographic.com/news/2004/12/1206_041206_global_warming.html

Rocky Mountain Climate Organization, www.rockymountainclimate.org/
Reports on the likely effects of global warming on the West

Spanish websites
www.cambioclimaticoglobal.com/
www.ceroco2.org/
www.ecoportal.net/temas/calenta.htm

U.S. Department of Energy, www.eia.doe.gov/kids/
General energy education for kids

www1.eere.energy.gov/kids/
Renewable energy and energy efficiency education for kids

California Energy Quest, www.energyquest.ca.gov/index.html
Interactive website for young people

Texas Energy Education Links
www.seco.cpa.state.tx.us/sch-gov_ed-links.htm
Web resources for young people

U.S. Department of Energy
Energy Efficiency Sites
www.eia.doe.gov/kids/energyfacts/saving/efficiency/savingenergy.html
www1.eere.energy.gov/kids/roofus/
www.ase.org/section/_audience/consumers/kids/
www.energyhog.org/childrens.htm

Solar Energy
www.eia.doe.gov/kids/energyfacts/sources/renewable/solar.html
www.solarenergy.org/resources/youngkids.html

www.solarenergy.org/resources/olderkids.html

www.energyquest.ca.gov/story/chapter15.html

Wind Energy

www.eia.doe.gov/kids/energyfacts/sources/renewable/wind.html

www.windpower.org/en/kids/index.htm

www.energyquest.ca.gov/story/chapter16.html

Biomass

www.eia.doe.gov/kids/energyfacts/sources/renewable/biomass.html

www.energyquest.ca.gov/story/chapter10.html

Geothermal

www.eia.doe.gov/kids/energyfacts/sources/renewable/geothermal.html

www1.eere.energy.gov/kids/geothermal.html

www.energyquest.ca.gov/story/chapter11.html

Hydro

www.eia.doe.gov/kids/energyfacts/sources/renewable/water.html

www.energyquest.ca.gov/story/chapter12.html

Nuclear

www.eia.doe.gov/kids/energyfacts/sources/non-renewable/nuclear.html

www.energyquest.ca.gov/story/chapter13.html

www.iter.org/

www.ucsusa.org/global_warming/solutions/nuclearandclimate.html

Hydrogen as Fuel

www.eia.doe.gov/kids/energyfacts/sources/IntermediateHydrogen.html

Glossary

active solar technology: A solar technology that requires an input of energy in order to get a larger output of energy.

advocate: A person who argues in favor of a particular position. In regard to energy, someone who favors a certain energy source.

Agricultural Revolution: The time during human pre-history when people discovered how to grow their own food.

agriculture: The science, art, and business of farming.

air-source heat pump: An electric-powered technology that makes use of a heat exchanger to heat and cool buildings.

algae: Simple green plants, most of which grow in water. In regard to energy, algae are a potential source of biodiesel.

appliance: An electrical device designed for a particular use in homes, businesses, or industry.

binary power plant: A geothermal power plant that allows warm water to produce electricity. The water transfers its heat to a second, or binary, fluid that boils at a lower temperature. This second fluid then produces the vapor that drives the turbine.

biodiesel: Diesel fuel made from a plant or an animal source rather than petroleum.

biofuel: Fuel made from a plant or an animal source rather than a fossil source.

cap and trade: An economic system that limits the amount of carbon emissions that can legally be produced (the cap) and requires polluters to buy and trade credits in order to be allowed to emit carbon up to this limit (the trade).

carbon: An element, number 8 on the periodic table, known as the building block of life because it is present in all life forms.

carbon capture and sequestration: A technology for capturing carbon dioxide before it leaves the stack of a power plant and burying it underground or removing it from circulation in some other way so it doesn't enter the atmosphere. This technology remains experimental.

carbon dioxide: A common compound consisting of one carbon atom and two oxygen atoms. Carbon dioxide is a gas that is released into the air whenever anything containing carbon is burned. It's a greenhouse gas, meaning that it absorbs the sun's heat and holds it in the atmosphere.

carbon neutral: A cycle that takes as much carbon out of the atmosphere as it puts in. For example, the life cycle of a plant is carbon neutral because the plant removes carbon from the air during its lifetime, then releases it during decomposition after death.

cellulosic ethanol: Ethanol produced from cellulose, the tough, woody part of plants.

centralization: Coming together, concentrating operations. In agriculture, the concentrating of farming operations into the hands of fewer farmers with larger farms.

climate: The long-term weather pattern of an area, including average temperatures, humidity, and precipitation.

coal: A soft black rock formed from the fossil remains of ancient plants. Coal is made almost entirely of carbon and is our most widely used fossil fuel.

compact fluorescent light (CFL): A bulb that uses fluorescent gases to produce light and consumes about of the energy of a standard incandescent bulb.

concentrating solar power (CSP): A form of solar-electric power. Concentrating solar power uses mirrors to focus sunlight on a central point. Fluid in this point is heated into vapor, turns a turbine, and produces electricity. Concentrating solar power is also known as solar-thermal power.

daylighting: The use of windows and skylights instead of electric lights.

dish Stirling system: A form of concentrating solar power.

economics: The social science that deals with the production, distribution, and consumption of goods and services.

efficiency: 1) How much of the energy resource is captured by the technology; 2) Doing the same amount of work with less energy wasted.

electricity: A form of kinetic energy resulting from the flow of electrons in a circuit.

energy: The capacity to do work.

energy conservation: Energy savings resulting from reduced use.

energy consumption: Energy use.

energy efficiency: The ratio of the energy output of a process to its energy input. Processes and technologies with higher efficiency put out more energy for the same input.

Energy Star: A U.S. government program that labels energy-efficient appliances.

ethanol: A form of alcohol that can substitute for gasoline as a fuel.

evaporative cooler: An air-conditioning technology that uses water to cool moving air; it works best in dry climates.

externality: An unintended consequence of an economic project felt outside the project itself and not included in the pricing or valuing of the project.

fault: In geology, a rock fracture that shows evidence of movement.

fertilizer: Natural or synthetic chemicals used to increase plant growth.

forecast: A long-term prediction of future behavior.

fossil fuels: Fuels from ancient carbon contained in the remains of fossil animals and plants. Coal, petroleum, and natural gas are fossil fuels.

fuel: Any material that is burned in order to get energy.

generating station: A power plant that produces electricity.

generator: A machine that produces electricity when turned by a turbine.

geologic plate: A rigid layer of the earth's crust that drifts slowly.

geothermal energy: Energy produced by using the earth's underground heat.

geothermal heat pump: A technology that makes use of the constant temperature several feet under the earth's surface to heat and cool buildings.

geothermal resource: The natural heat, steam, and hot water within the earth.

global warming: An increase in the greenhouse effect that leads to warmer average temperatures around the world.

greenhouse effect: The action of certain gases in the atmosphere that absorb the sun's energy and raise the temperature of the atmosphere.

grid: In regard to electricity, the network of transmission lines that carry electricity from its source to its point of use.

grid tied: Wired into the electric grid.

ground source heat pump: Another name for a geothermal heat pump.

heliostats: A mirror that follows the movement of the sun and reflects its light onto a fixed point. Used as a part of concentrating solar power systems.

herbicide: A natural or synthetic chemical used to kill unwanted plants.

hot dry rock: A geothermal technology for producing electricity in areas with accessible underground heat but no hot water.

hot spots: Areas of the earth where underground heat, hot water, and/or steam come close to the surface.

hydrofraccing: Cracking rock by forcing water into it under high pressure.

hydrogen: The lightest element, number 1 on the periodic table. Hydrogen can be burned cleanly, emitting only water as a by-product. However, it's a difficult fuel to produce and to store.

hydrogen economy: A vision of an energy future in which hydrogen fuel cells are the main source of fuel.

incandescent bulb: The original electric lightbulb, which produces light with a metal filament that, when connected to an electric current, gets so hot it glows.

Industrial Revolution: The time in history, during the 1800s, when factories and machines replaced hand tools and industry developed rapidly.

industry: The organized action of making goods and services for sale.

intermittency: Occurring at some times and not at others.

internal combustion engine: An engine that burns fuel inside a combustion chamber and converts it into motion. This is the original engine used to power the automobile.

isotopes: Atoms with the same number of protons and electrons but different numbers of neutrons.

kilowatt-hour: The work performed by one kilowatt of electric power in one hour. The unit on which the price of electrical energy is based.

kinetic energy: The energy of a moving object.

light-emitting diode (LED): A semiconductor that transmits light into a fiber in response to an electric signal.

magma: Molten rock.

mantle: The layer of the earth just under the crust.

mechanization: The use of machinery to replace human or animal labor.

natural gas: Deposits of gases, mostly methane, found underground where carbon-based materials have decomposed under pressure. Burned as fossil fuel.

nuclear energy: The energy stored in the nucleus of an atom.

nuclear fission: The splitting of an atom's nucleus into two or more parts.

nuclear fusion: Two atomic nuclei coming together to form a single, larger nucleus.

nuclear meltdown: Severe overheating of the core of a nuclear reactor, resulting in the core melting and radiation escaping.

nuclear reactor: The part of a nuclear power plant where the nuclear fission activity takes place.

nuclear weapons: Weapons that use chain reactions of nuclear fission and/or fusion to cause large-scale destruction.

organic: In chemistry, meaning containing carbon. In agriculture, meaning a process of raising food without using synthetic pesticides, herbicides, fertilizers, or hormones.

parabolic trough: A form of concentrating solar power that makes use of long curved mirrors.

passive solar design: Techniques that use the sun's energy directly to heat, cool, and light buildings.

pesticide: A synthetic or natural chemical that kills pests that prey on crops.

petroleum: A liquid fossil fuel formed from the remains of tiny marine animals. Also called crude oil. Gasoline, diesel, asphalt, and plastics are made from petroleum.

photosynthesis: The chemical process used by green plants to convert the sun's energy into stored energy, which they use to live and grow.

photovoltaic panels: Solar-electric panels, which produce electricity from sunlight.

potential energy: The energy stored in an object.

power tower: A form of concentrating solar power in which many mirrors reflect sunlight onto a central point.

radioactivity: The release of particles and energy from the unstable nucleus of an atom.

refrigerated air: A form of air conditioning that removes heat from a building by using a heat exchanger containing compressed gas that absorbs heat and releases it to the outdoors. The technology is very similar to a refrigerator's.

renewable energy: Energy from a source that naturally renews itself. Solar, wind, and geothermal are all renewable sources because they can't be used up.

saline aquifer: A salty underground water source.

sector: In economics, a part of the economy. For example, the agricultural sector, the industrial sector, the business sector.

self-contained: In regard to solar-electric systems, systems that do not need to be connected to the electrical grid.

solar energy: Energy from the sun.

solar home: A home using passive solar design to provide heat and light.

solar thermal: Heat energy produced directly from sunlight.

solar thermal plant: Another name for a concentrating solar plant.

solid state lighting: Another term for light-emitting diodes and related technologies.

steam engine: A machine invented in 1712 that turns fuel into mechanical energy. A coal fire heats water, which produces steam. The pressure of the steam raises and lowers pistons that can turn wheels, operate pumps, or hammers, and so on. Development of the steam engine led to the Industrial Revolution.

Stirling engine: A form of concentrating solar power.

swamp cooler: A common name for evaporative coolers.

thermal mass: The ability of an object to store heat. In passive solar design, building materials used to absorb the sun's heat during the day and release it at night.

thermal storage: Storage of energy as heat, in a material of high thermal mass.

transmission: In regard to electricity, the process of transporting electrical energy from one point to another in the power system.

transmission line: A power line used to carry large amounts of electrical energy, usually over long distances.

turbine: A machine used in the production of electricity. It has blades attached to a central shaft. The pressure of water or steam on these blades causes the turbine to spin, rotating a component in a generator that converts the mechanical energy into electricity.

uranium: The heaviest element found in nature, number 92 on the periodic table. Uranium is naturally unstable and radioactive.

wind farm: An array of wind turbines.

wind turbine: A turbine that makes electricity from wind energy.

yield: In agriculture, the amount of harvest produced by a given piece of land.

Illustration Credits

page x, vi	© PhotoDisc by Getty Images
page 1	Missy Cook, Center for Excellence in Hazardous Materials Management
page 2	Sandia National Laboratories
page 4	Geothermal Education Office, Tiburon, CA
page 5	© iStockphoto.com
page 7	Catherine Paplin
page 8	Geothermal Education Office, Tiburon, CA
page 8	Geothermal Education Office, Tiburon, CA
page 9	© iStockphoto.com
page 10	Eva Thaddeus
page 13	Los Alamos National Laboratory
page 14	Eva Thaddeus
page 15	Catherine Paplin
page 17	© Printroom.com Photography
page 19	Eva Thaddeus
page 20	Los Alamos National Laboratory
page 21	Los Alamos National Laboratory
page 22	© Artville
page 24	Catherine Paplin
page 27	© iStockphoto.com
page 28	Sandia National Laboratories
page 30	NASA
page 32	Catherine Paplin
page 34	NASA
page 35	Chris Carter
page 36	Geothermal Education Office, Tiburon, CA
page 37	Geothermal Education Office, Tiburon, CA

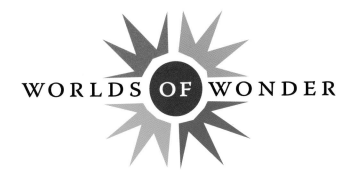

WORLDS OF WONDER

Welcome to

Worlds of Wonder

A Young Reader's Science Series

Advisory Editors: David Holtby and Karen Taschek

In these engagingly written and beautifully illustrated books, the University of New Mexico Press seeks to convey to young readers the thrill of science as well as to inspire further inquiry into the wonders of scientific research and discovery.

ALSO AVAILABLE IN THE BARBARA GUTH WORLDS OF WONDER SERIES:

Hanging with Bats: Ecobats, Vampires, and Movie Stars
by Karen Taschek

The Tree Rings' Tale: Understanding Our Changing Climate
by John Fleck

Global Warming and Climate Change by Chuck McCutcheon

Index

agriculture, 5, 82–88
  Agricultural Revolution, 16
  local, 85
  organic, 84, 87
air conditioning, 76–77, 91
algae, 1, 95–99
atomic bomb, 12, 13, 19
automobile, 18, 79

Baer, Steve, 65–67
Bandelier National Monument, 14, 15
Beauchamp, Helene, 67–69
Berman, Marshall, 26–28
binary power plant, 44
biofuels, 92–99
  biodiesel, 1, 95–99
  bioethanol, 92–94
Brazil, 99
buildings, 5, 15, 73–79
Bustos, Don, 87–89

cap and trade, 104
carbon capture and sequestration, 102–3
carbon dioxide, 6, 7–8, 28, 78, 92, 102–4
Carlsbad, 96
Chaco Canyon, 16
China, 8, 33, 85–86
climate, 6–9, 50, 66
coal, 5, 6, 17, 28, 50, 78, 104
concentrating solar power, 53–57

electric car, 80
electricity, 3, 23, 29, 34, 39, 41, 51, 57, 76, 91
  electric appliances, 5
  "the grid," 3, 39, 51–52, 59
energy
  conservation, 71–72
  consumption, 71
  efficiency, 64, 71–89
Energy Information Agency, 71
Energy Star, 77
externality, 6, 7, 9, 25, 33

Fenton Hill, 42–45
fire, 14, 16

food, 3, 5, 13–14, 16, 82–88
fossil fuels, 4–9, 40, 42, 47, 88,
    93, 104
France, 30, 33

generator, 23, 39
geothermal energy, 35–47, 71
    geothermal heat pump, 46–47
    geothermal resource, 39, 40, 41
Germany, 69
global warming, 6–9, 28, 91
Goff, Fraser, 44–45
greenhouse effect, 7
ground source heat pump,
    46–47, 76

Hanley, Charles, 1–2, 10, 58–60
Hill, Roger, 47
hot dry rock, 42–45
hot spot, 37
hydrogen
    bomb, 21
    fuel, 29, 101–2
    nuclear fusion and, 31–32
    sun and, 31–32

Iceland, 39, 42
Indonesia, 95
Industrial Revolution, 17–18
Israel, 67
ITER, 33

Japan, 30, 33, 72, 73, 89

Kelly, John, 29–30, 34

lightbulb, 77–79
Los Alamos, 19–22, 37

Malaysia, 95
Mancini, Tom, 53–57
Mazria, Ed, 73–75, 79
methane, 88

National Aeronautics and Space
    Administration (NASA), 29–30
natural gas, 5, 50, 88
New Mexico, 1, 10, 11, 13, 18–22, 38,
    96
New Mexico Wind Energy Center,
    62–64
nuclear energy, 23–34
    nuclear bomb, 11–13, 19–21
    nuclear fission, 23, 24, 32
    nuclear fusion, 31–33
    nuclear power, 23–34, 69, 71
    nuclear reactor, 23, 25–28, 34
    nuclear waste, 25, 30
Oppenheimer, J. Robert, 12, 20

petroleum, 5, 79, 91, 104
Philippines, 42, 47
photosynthesis, 49, 96
photovoltaics, 51, 55, 58–60
pollution, 6, 28, 78, 91, 102

radioactivity, 23–25, 30, 36
renewable energy, 40, 52, 64, 69,
    88
Ring of Fire, 37

Sandia National Laboratories, 1, 26,
    29, 58
Seibel, Tom, 85–87
solar energy, 14–15, 49–69
    active, 52
    indirect, 49
    passive, 16, 51, 66
    solar-electric panels, 58–60
    solar hot water, 51, 67–68
    solar thermal, 55, 65, 87–88
Southwestern United States,
    12, 13
spacecraft, 29, 34
Spain, 69
Stroud, Wren, 1–2, 10, 95–99, 105

thermal storage, 55–56, 76
thin-film solar cells, 61–62
transmission lines, 5, 60
transportation, 5, 79–82, 91
   hydrogen fuel and, 29
   public, 81
Trinity Site, 11–13
turbine, 23, 39, 52, 62–63

uranium, 23–25, 28
utilities, 55

wind energy, 50, 62–64, 69, 71
wind farm, 40, 62–64